Southeast Asia

New and Future Titles in the Indigenous Peoples of the World Include:

Australia
Gypsies
Pacific Islands
Southeast Asia

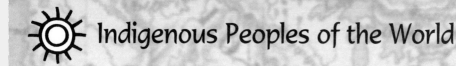
Southeast Asia

Mary C. Wilds

LUCENT
BOOKS ®

THOMSON
———— ✦ ———— ™
GALE

San Diego • Detroit • New York • San Francisco • Cleveland • New Haven, Conn. • Waterville, Maine • London • Munich

LIBRARY OF CONGRESS CATALOGING-IN-PUBLICATION DATA

Wilds, Mary C., 1960-
　　Southeast Asia / by Mary C. Wilds.
　　　　p. cm. — (Indigenous peoples of the world)
　Includes bibliographical references and index.
　　ISBN 1-59018-095-X (hardback : alk. paper)
　　1. Asia, Southeastern—Juvenile literature I. Title. II. Series.
　DS521 .W53 2003
　959—dc21

　　　　　　　　　　　　　　　　　　　　　　　　　　　　　　2002007295

Printed in the United States of America

Contents

Foreword

Nearly every area of the world has indigenous populations, those people who are descended from the original settlers of a given region, often arriving many millennia ago. Many of these populations exist today despite overwhelming odds against their continuing survival.

Though indigenous populations have come under attack for a variety of reasons, in most cases land lies at the heart of the conflict. The hunger for land has threatened indigenous societies throughout history, whether the aggressor was a neighboring tribe or a foreign culture. The reason for this is simple: For indigenous populations, *way of life* has nearly always depended on the land and its bounty. Indeed, cultures from the Inuit of the frigid Arctic to the Yanomami of the torrid Amazon rain forest have been indelibly shaped by the climate and geography of the regions they inhabit.

As newcomers moved into already settled areas of the world, competition led to tension and violence. When newcomers possessed some important advantage—greater numbers or more powerful weapons—the results were predictable. History is rife with examples of outsiders triumphing over indigenous populations. Anglo-Saxons and Vikings, for instance, moved into eastern Europe and the British Isles at the expense of the indigenous Celts. Europeans traveled south through Africa and into Australia displacing the indigenous Bushmen and Aborigines while other Westerners ventured into the Pacific at the expense of the indigenous Melanesians, Micronesians, and Polynesians. And in North and South America, the colonization of the New World by European powers resulted in the decimation and displacement of numerous Native American groups.

Nevertheless, many indigenous populations retained their identity and managed to survive. Only in the last one hundred years, however, have anthropologists begun to study with any objectivity the hundreds of indigenous societies found throughout the world. And only within the last few decades have these societies been truly appreciated and acknowledged for their richness and complexity. The ability to adapt to and manage their environments is but one marker of the incredible resourcefulness of many indigenous populations. The Inuit, for example, created two distinct modes of travel for getting around the barren, icy region that is their home. The sleek, speedy kayak—with its whalebone frame and sealskin cover—allowed the Inuit to silently skim the waters of the nearby ocean and bays. And the sledge (or dogsled)—with its caribou hide platform and runners built from whalebone or frozen fish covered with sealskin—made travel over the snow- and ice-covered landscape possible.

The Indigenous Peoples of the World series strives to present a clear and realistic picture of the world's many and varied native cultures. The series captures the uniqueness as well as the similarities of indigenous societies by examining family and community life, traditional spirituality and religion, warfare, adaptation to the environment, and interaction with other native and nonnative peoples.

The series also offers perspective on the effects of Western civilization on indigenous populations as well as a multifaceted view of contemporary life. Many indigenous societies, for instance, struggle today with poverty, unemployment, racism, poor health, and a lack of educational opportunities. Others find themselves embroiled in political instability, civil unrest, and violence. Despite the problems facing these societies, many indigenous populations have regained a sense of pride in themselves and their heritage. Many also have experienced a resurgence of traditional art and culture as they seek to find a place for themselves in the modern world.

The Indigenous Peoples of the World series offers an in-depth study of different regions of the world and the people who have long inhabited those regions. All books in the series include fully documented primary and secondary source quotations that enliven the text. Sidebars highlight notable events, personalities, and traditions, while annotated bibliographies offer ideas for future research. Numerous maps and photographs provide the reader with a pictorial glimpse of each society.

From the Aborigines of Australia to the various indigenous peoples of the Caribbean, Europe, South America, Mexico, Asia, and Africa, the series covers a multitude of societies and their cultures. Each book stands alone and the series as a collection offers valuable comparisons of the past history and future problems of the indigenous peoples of the world.

A Region's Geography Shapes Its People

The indigenous peoples of Southeast Asia have been marked not only by the region's hot and humid climate but also by its rough and rugged terrain. Those nations on the mainland—Vietnam, Cambodia, Laos, Myanmar (formerly Burma), and Thailand—are laced with formidable rivers and vast mountain ranges. The others, all islands and island chains—Indonesia, Malaysia, Brunei, Singapore, and the Philippines—are bracketed by thousands of miles of typhoon-infested seas.

Anthropologists believe that the region's geography both helped and hurt early humans who settled Southeast Asia. For example, the mainland rivers, which mostly run south from Tibet and China, served as traffic arteries; people used them to travel from place to place by boat. In contrast, the mountain ranges—described by one historian as "the arms of an octopus" reaching across a continent—served as walls. They were so impassable that they tended to isolate the peoples who lived between them.

The island nations are equally isolated, separated as they are by so much ocean. The sheer number of islands in the region tended to keep tribes from interacting with one another. Indonesia's island chain is made up of more than 17,000 small islands, totaling 741,052 square miles. The Philippines has 7 major islands and 7,100 minor ones—300,000 square miles of land mass total.

When groups of humans who live in the same region are isolated from one another for so many years, each group tends to develop its own unique language and culture; hence the rich variety of indigenous cultures and traditions in the Southeast Asia region. A good example of the effect that isolation can have on culture is the Asmat people, who live in the swamp regions of Indonesia. The Asmat were once fierce headhunters but today are known for their skilled artwork and woodcarving. When the Asmat were discovered by Westerners, more than two hundred separate languages were observed between the tribal groups. Because Asmat groups had so little contact with each other, they developed different languages even though all belonged to the same tribe.

The First Peoples

It is believed that the first wave of human migration occurred in the region be-cause a land bridge connected the continent to the islands many thousands of years ago. The earliest humans settled in China and Tibet and then, more than ten thousand years ago, began a southward migration into Southeast Asia. These early humans lived as hunter-gatherers until about 3000 B.C., when rice growing

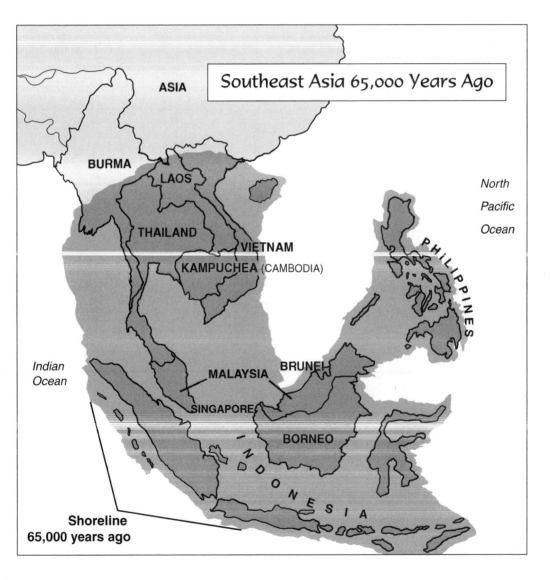

Southeast Asia 65,000 Years Ago

ASIA

BURMA

LAOS

THAILAND

VIETNAM

KAMPUCHEA (CAMBODIA)

North Pacific Ocean

PHILIPPINES

Indian Ocean

MALAYSIA

BRUNEI

SINGAPORE

BORNEO

INDONESIA

Shoreline 65,000 years ago

and irrigation techniques arrived in the region. By 2000 B.C., they were making metal weapons and tools.

A subgroup of early settlers, the Austronesians, adapted well to the sea and migrated eastward into the region's island nations about four thousand years ago. Many Filipino tribes can now trace their ancestry back to the Austronesians. Another group known as the Proto-Malay originally lived in Vietnam, but were crowded out by tribes migrating from China about seven thousand years ago. Also a seafaring people, the Proto-Malay migrated to Malaysia, Sumatra, and Bor-neo. The Proto-Malay were the descendants of such modern-day indigenous tribes as the Dyak, Bajau, and Kazadan.

Most mainland tribes can trace their ancestry back to China, Tibet, or India. The Mons of Burma are believed to have migrated from southwestern China. Both the Karen and Chin tribes may have originated in eastern Tibet; both also live in Burma. The Khmer arrived in Cambodia from either southwest China or India around 2000 B.C. As tribespeople moved south and eastward across the continent, many chose to settle in more than one region. Thus, as national borders formed, tribes found

A group of Karen women and children. The Karen tribe may have descended from Tibetan ancestors.

themselves in several different countries. Today, members of the Karen live in a mountainous region that straddles both Burma and Thailand. Hmong tribespeople, who also come from China, live in the highlands of Laos, Vietnam, and Thailand.

On the island nations, however, there are pockets of peoples here and there who have no genetic link to the mainland. These tribes, who include the Negritos, are believed to have originated among the Pacific Island chains themselves.

Close to the Earth

Those who settled Southeast Asia did not have the kinds of tools that would change the landscape to suit their needs. They had to develop a lifestyle and culture suitable to the terrain and climate in which they lived. The indigenous tribes that live in the region today developed from these early peoples, and they, too, have a traditional lifestyle that is uniquely suited to the land and climate in which they live.

Chapter 1

The Tribes of Southeast Asia

To understand daily life in Southeast Asia, one must first understand the weather. The hot, humid, and wet weather of the region has shaped the way its native peoples grow their crops, build their homes, and live their daily lives.

Of Rice and Rain

The weather of Southeast Asia is controlled by monsoon winds, which are one of the most massive weather systems in the world. These winds rotate between India, Southeast Asia, Australia, and the oceans of the region. In Southeast Asia, monsoon winds blow from the southwest from May through September, bringing heavy rains. In the winter they blow from the northeast, bringing cool, dry air onto the continent and the surrounding islands. (Of all the Southeast Asian nations, only Indonesia is an exception to this rule: Like Australia, its rainy season begins in the winter.)

The heavy rains of spring and summer—coupled with the region's hot and humid climate—restrict the kinds of crops that can be grown; the vegetation that naturally grows in the region; the species of animals that live in the forests, plains, and mountains; and the lifestyles of the people. But the indigenous tribes of the region have learned to live within the ebb and flow of their environment. Most built their homes on a raised platform, supported by either wooden or bamboo poles, as a defense against sudden floods that might wash away all they have. They cultivated rice, a plant that thrives in shallow water.

They foraged and hunted in rain forests, jungles, and coastal plains that were home to some of the world's most unique plant and animal species, including the tiger, the dwarf buffalo, and the Asian elephant, to name a few.

The Hill Tribes

Indigenous populations in the region currently number in the millions, with the nation of Myanmar, traditionally known as Burma, first on the list with about 10 million tribespeople—Karen, Chin, Kachin,

Palung, Shan, and others who made up about 30 percent of the population in 1992 (the year from which the most recent data are available).

Also in 1992, roughly fifty Filipino groups made up 16 percent of the popula-tion: the Bontoc, Bangsa Moro, Ibaloi, Kalinga, Ifuago, Kankanai, and others, most of whom live in the Cordillera region of Luzon (the northern half of the main island) and the forests of Mindanao. On the Malaysian mainland, 4 percent of

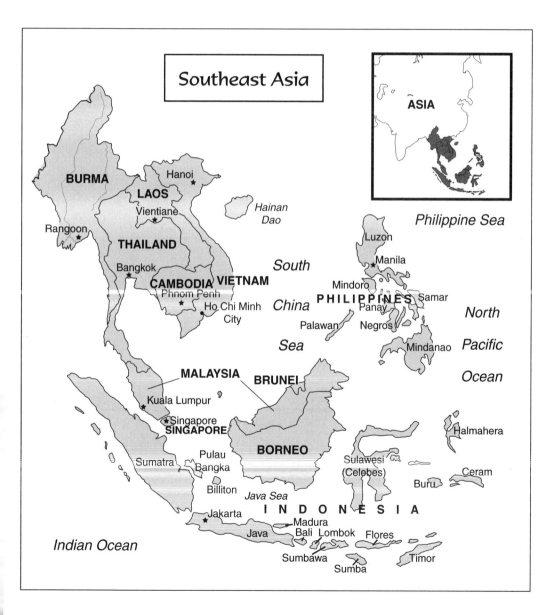

A Dyak woman from Borneo.

tively isolated locations has allowed hill tribespeople to pursue their traditional culture and practice their religion. Some tribes, like Vietnam's Montagnard, retreated to the highlands to escape prejudice. Montagnard tribespeople were frequently ostracized by their fellow inhabitants because of their comparatively dark skin color; lowlanders referred to them as the Meori, or dark-skinned ones.

Dividing Southeast Asia's indigenous peoples into two groups, farmers and hunter-gatherers, is a good way to study them. Farming tribes depend not only on crops but also on hunting, trapping, fishing, and raising livestock for their livelihood. Most modern-day farming tribes tend to have some contact with the outside world, and some even cater to the tourist trade.

Hunter-gatherers, who get their food entirely from hunting, fishing, and the gathering of edible plants and herbs from the forest, tend to move from place to place within a large area. Southeast Asian hunter-gatherer tribes are threatened by residential development, mining, large-scale farming, and deforestation in their homelands. Today their numbers are much smaller than the agrarian tribes.

the population is indigenous, while in Sabah and Sarawak, the two eastern states that occupy the northern half of the island of Borneo, fully half of the population is indigenous. These peoples include the Iban, Dyak, Kayan, and Penan. Thailand is home to nine tribal groups including the Hmong and Karen, and in Vietnam, Laos, and Cambodia, about 1 million tribespeople still known as Montagnard make their home.

Almost without exception, Southeast Asia's indigenous peoples live in the highlands of their respective nations; thus they are known as "hill tribes." Living in rela-

A Tradition of Growing Rice

The majority of the region's indigenous peoples do at least some farming, generally by means of a centuries-old agricultural technique called swidden, also known as slash and burn. When practicing swidden, tribespeople will select hillside fields near their village and clear them by cutting and burning away brush, trees, and grasses. Rice is cultivated on the site, and after the harvest the tribe abandons it for another field, upon which the same swidden technique is performed. While the original fields lie fallow, the brush, grasses, and small trees begin to grow on it again. Soon the new plants return nutrients to the soil that the crops used up. After several years, the fields will be ready again for cultivation.

In 1972, *National Geographic* writer Peter Kunstadter visited Karen tribespeople in Thailand and witnessed a swidden burn:

The Khmer Kingdom

The region of Southeast Asia has produced some of the most glittering cultures the world has ever known. One of the most influential of these was the Khmer empire, the descendants of which still live in Cambodia today. The actual kingdom encompassed modern-day Laos and Cambodia, parts of Thailand, and the Mekong region of Vietnam. Its golden age peaked between the years A.D. 889 to 1434.

The Khmer attracted numerous Indian scholars, artists, and religious teachers to its court, and these foreign thinkers had a huge impact on Khmer culture. They worshiped the Hindu gods and learned Sanskrit, one of the world's oldest written languages. The Khmers did have their own literature, but their greatest achievements are in sculpture and architecture, particularly the art form known as bas-relief.

A bas-relief artist etches images onto a flat stone surface, usually a wall. The images are raised, but not three-dimensional; they are like paintings in stone. Using this technique, a talented artist can cover a large area

and depict very detailed scenes. Khmer artists used the technique to depict scenes of daily life in their kingdom.

Like most kingdoms of their era, the Khmer fought repeated wars with their neighbors. They frequently battled the Assamese, from a region that fringes India and Myanmar, and the Cham, who founded Champa, another great Southeast Asian empire. In the twelfth century the Khmer raided Champa, only to be sacked in return by the Cham, who invaded the Khmer's capital, Angkor, located in what is now modern-day Cambodia. Two hundred years later the Khmer had a new foe: Thailand.

The Thai repeatedly attacked the Khmer, weakening their armies and their power. They captured Angkor in 1434 and forcibly moved Cambodia's capital to Phnom Penh. The Khmer remained in Cambodia, where their descendants still live, but the brilliance of their civilization can be discerned now mainly from the ruins and rare, preserved works of art that archaeologists have uncovered.

The men lit the first fires at the tops of the fields, helping create an updraft to assure a quick, complete burn. Firebreaks that had been cleared previously kept the flames from spreading over the ridgetops. . . . A few people stayed home to guard the village houses. [A villager] climbed to the ridgepole of his house carrying water-filled bamboo tubes. Taking big mouthfuls of the water, he sprayed the thatch to keep it damp and cool. . . . In about an hour more than a hundred acres were reduced to bare hillsides.[1]

Tools of the indigenous farmer are always simple and handmade. They include goosenecked cutting instruments, known by the Vietnamese as *chuang,* used to split wood and fell trees; knives, or *chang,* used for carving; and *maks,* which resemble scythes and are used to clear fields. Actual cultivation techniques are both simple and complex. At one end of the spectrum is the tribesman-planter, walking across a cleared hillside, armed with only a sharpened or metal-tipped wooden stick. The planter uses the stick to poke holes in the soil, and plants the season's rice crop hole by hole, seed by seed. (Indigenous tribespeople do not use plows because they believe that plowing would disturb the spirits living in the ground.) At the other end of the spectrum is the entire tribe building flat-topped rice terraces along a hillside. Rice and other crops are grown atop the terraces, which resemble stair steps.

The most spectacular example of the rice terrace can still be seen in the Luzon region of the Philippines. Dubbed as the Eighth Wonder of the World by early explorers, the rice terraces of the Ifuago tribe, built more than one thousand years ago, cover whole mountainsides and are still in use today. The rice is irrigated by man-made ditches of considerable length. The terrace walls are mostly made of stone and stand between ten and forty feet high. The tribespeople also built their homes beside the terrace walls, as a safeguard for the crops and the villagers.

Perhaps the most unusual cultivation method of all can be found at Inle Lake in northern Burma, located northeast of Rangoon in the mountains of the Shan region. Inle Lake is eighteen miles long and five miles wide. It is home to the Mon tribes (who are a different group from the Hmong, although the names are similar), and its shores support about two hundred villages with a total population of about 150,000. These Inle Lake Mon are known as the Intha, which mean "sons of the lake." The Intha have come up with an ingenious method of farming within the lake itself. They weave rubbery tubes of water hyacinths and rushes (both of which grow naturally in Inle Lake) together into gigantic nets. They then dredge mud from the lake bottom and spread a layer of humus on the nets. These floating gardens are staked near the family home with wood or bamboo poles.

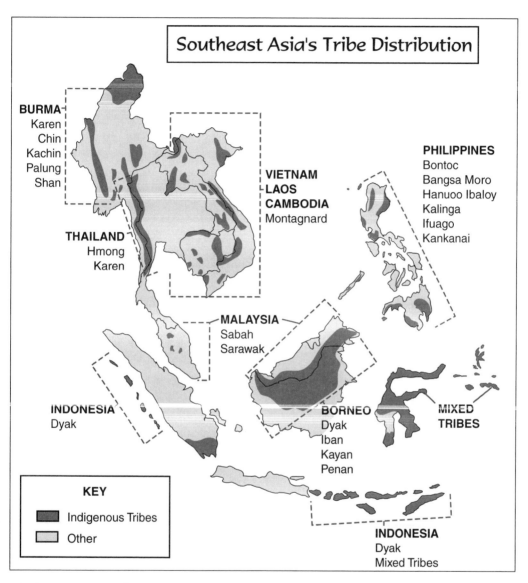

Southeast Asia's Tribe Distribution

BURMA
Karen
Chin
Kachin
Palung
Shan

THAILAND
Hmong
Karen

VIETNAM
LAOS
CAMBODIA
Montagnard

PHILIPPINES
Bontoc
Bangsa Moro
Hanuoo Ibaloy
Kalinga
Ifuago
Kankanai

MALAYSIA
Sabah
Sarawak

INDONESIA
Dyak

BORNEO
Dyak
Iban
Kayan
Penan

MIXED
TRIBES

INDONESIA
Dyak
Mixed Tribes

KEY

■ Indigenous Tribes
□ Other

Other Crops for Sustenance and Construction

Rice may be Southeast Asia's most important crop, but it is not the only one. Tribespeople on both the mainland and island nations grow hemp and cotton, which they use to make clothing. The Ifuago tribespeople of the Philippines grow not only rice on their magnificent terraces, but also beans, onions, and gobi, or taro, which is an edible tuber, like a potato. Highland regions tend to be much drier than the lowlands; hence the great variety of crops. The Vietnamese Hmong, who number more than four hundred thousand individuals in eleven provinces, tend fruit orchards alongside their rice and hemp fields. Plums, peaches, and apples grown by the Hmong are prized throughout the country, although transportation problems in the country make selling the produce difficult. The Ra De, who live in the Vietnamese province of Dak Lak and are a subgroup of the Montagnard people, grow melons, cotton, tobacco, and sugar cane. The sugar cane is used to make wine rather than baked goods, soft drinks, and candy as in the West. Coffee is also grown in Vietnam but is confined mostly to commercial plantations. Coffee was introduced in the region many years ago by Westerners who wished to export it.

These agrarian tribes have a good deal in common with one another. Most live in permanent villages in the valleys or on hillsides near the crops they raise. They build their homes from bamboo, a plentiful plant on both the mainland and islands. On the mainland both the roofs and walls are constructed from bamboo; on the island tribespeople are more likely to thatch their roofs with leaves from the species of palm that grow in that region. Villagers also like to build near water sources, a preference that may have resulted in the practice of raising houses on wooden or bamboo poles.

Livestock

No indigenous farmer relies solely on crops for sustenance. Beneath the raised platform of most houses is a place to keep pigs and chickens; like their counterparts on small family farms in the West, villages get protein from eggs and meat. But here the similarity ends: Instead of dairy cows and sheep, the Southeast Asian farmer keeps water buffalo and, rarely, an Asian elephant.

The Asian elephant has a long and colorful history on that continent: First domesticated around 2000 B.C., it carried kings into battle and helped its masters clear forests with the help of its strong trunk. Its African counterpart accompanied Hannibal on his ill-fated march across the Alps. Today, however, the domesticated Asian elephant is used for heavy tasks, like hauling timber, or for giving rides to the tourists who flock to Southeast Asia from Europe, the United States, Taiwan, and Japan. Very few indigenous tribes actually own an elephant, however, because they are so expensive to maintain.

The water buffalo is a different story. Also known as the Asiatic buffalo, this two-thousand-pound member of the wild ox family has been a beast of burden in Southeast Asia for thousands of years. The Bajau of Belud, a region of Sabah (on the eastern side of the island of Borneo), keep whole herds of buffalo much the same way that American ranchers keep cattle. They tend their herds on horseback and are such highly skilled horsemen that they are known as the cowboys of the East. These "cowboys" are often invited to appear in state-sponsored celebrations, riding mounts decked out with tiny bells, colorful reins, and cloths.

The Hmong and the Poppy

The Hmong have always been a highly accomplished people. They tell rich and highly imaginative folktales; they weave and sew beautiful native costumes. But the Hmong have another, more controversial tradition: the growing of poppy flowers, which they then convert to opium. Opium is used in several ways by the Hmong. It is smoked socially, but addiction is frowned upon, and addicts bring shame and dishonor to their families. They also use opium to treat illness, such as dysentery and tuberculosis. Opium is also used to trade for precious metals and buffalo, which are in turn used by Hmong families in their marriage rituals.

The Hmong live in China, Laos, and Vietnam. About fifty-eight thousand of them live in an area of Thailand known as the golden triangle—the largest growing area for opium in the world. But Hmong who live in Thailand and elsewhere have long been pressured to stop this tradition, in the interest of stopping drug traffic, the largest market for which is the United States. Yet the take from the opium crop is very small compared with thousands of dollars made by other people on the drug provider chain. Moreover, the Hmong of Thailand have been asked to plant other crops, but the species suggested are susceptible to bad weather and fluctuating prices.

The Hmong of Vietnam, however, have become powerful enough that some of their members have served in that country's national assembly. Hence, Vietnamese officials have treaded much more lightly in their efforts to stamp out the opium crop in their country. In 1996 the government and the United Nations (UN) agreed to pump more than $4 million into the Ky Son district, a Hmong stronghold, in an effort to wean local farmers from opium growing. The UN's Drug Control Program (UNDCP) also advises Vietnam on the creation of armed border task forces to tackle dealers and traffickers. Meanwhile, Vietnam must also cope with its own population of opium addicts, many of whom live in urban areas.

The Cowboys Who Came In from the Sea

These Bajau were once part of a larger tribal band known as the Sea Gypsies, for good reason. For generations the Bajau, or Sea Gypsies, roamed the islands of Malaysia, the Philippines, and Indonesia, dwelling in harbor villages or on their *lipas* (boats), living on batches of tuna, shark, stingray, and anything else they could take from the sea. A Bajau family interviewed by *National Geographic* writer Anne de Henning Singh describes the hazards of the old days: "[A tribeswoman] told me that once her brother and father were caught in

A man directs an Asian elephant from atop its back. Elephants have a long history as work animals in Asia.

a storm and drifted a hundred miles to Borneo. 'They were gone two months and we thought they were dead,' she said."[2]

Changing economic conditions, religious conflicts in the region, commercial fishing, and even raids by pirates forced Bajau groups ashore. Those tribes, however, still keep their connection to the sea. They build their homes on stilts along the shoreline, with boardwalks over the water that connect them with their neighbors. And many Bajau children still learn to swim before they can walk.

Traditional Ways to Hunt and Fish

The Bajau fish the way Western fisherman do: over the side of the boat with baited lines. Other tribes, like the Intha Mon, prefer spears and nets. When they go fishing the Inthas bring a cone-shaped net, a spear, a boat, and an oar. With one leg wrapped around the oar, the fisherman propels the boat through the water, keeping an eye out for schools of fish. Once one is spotted, he drops the net, traps the fish, and spears them.

The Intha Mon are not known to hunt, but many other agrarian tribes do. Deer, wild pig, and pheasant are favorite game animals in the region, and tribal hunters bring them down with traps, spears, crossbows, and, in some island regions, blowpipes.

The Senoi tribe of peninsular Malaysia are artists when it comes to the blowpipe. The Senoi are a subgroup of the Orang Asli, thought to be the oldest group of inhabitants in Malaysia. The Senoi, who are also rice growers, traditionally hunt with intricately carved bamboo blowpipes that measure about six feet long. The Senoi "blow" darts tipped with sap from poisonous trees like the *ipoh*. The blowpipes are known for their deadly accuracy; skilled users can hit targets as far away as twenty-four feet.

A Well-Studied Tribe of Hunter-Gatherers

Hunter-gatherer tribes are most often found on the island nations of Malaysia, the Philippines, and Indonesia, and their lifestyle is very different from that of the agrarian tribespeople. Hunter-gatherers do not keep domestic animals and rarely have permanent homes. Their clothing is simple,

though body ornamentation and jewelry can be quite ornate.

One of the more well studied of the hunter-gatherers—as well as one of the most threatened—are the Penan of Malaysia, who occupy the interior of Sarawak's rain forest. Less than five hundred of them still practice their traditional way of life; others have been lured away by farming or by jobs with the logging and tourism industries.

"[Those who have left the forest] are either settled or semisettled in upriver villages, where they are learning to farm hill rice, bananas and tapioca," writes Eric Hansen, who visited the Penan in 1998 and profiled them in an article for *Natural History*. "Many of the Penan go to church on Sundays, some of their children attend government schools and most wear Western-style clothing."[3]

Those Penan who still practice their traditional ways are expert foragers, plucking jackfruit (which is like a large pear), wild honey, rattan, giant bamboo, edible ferns and birds' nests, tree resin, and sago palm, one of their staple foods, from the rain forest. Penan traditionally traded some of these items for salt, tobacco, iron tools, and fabric, though today's tribespeople, even those who still live in the forest, are just as likely to trade for wristwatches and sunglasses.

Penan are also hunters, taking advantage of wild pig and several species of deer native to the rain forest. Their forest shelters are simple, constructed of wooden poles set upright in the earth and roofed by palm leaves. "The Penan have an expression: 'From the forest we get our life,'"

Penan men building a temporary shelter. The Penan tribe lives off what the forest provides.

Hansen wrote. "They did not overexploit their environment, and for this reason the plant, fish, and animal populations in their part of the forest remained stable until recently."[4] Hansen also points out that, contrary to conventional wisdom, the Penan do not wander the forest aimlessly:

> Traditionally their movements were carefully thought out, and they followed a network of well-established trails that connected stands of wild sago palms and areas rich in fish and game. In addition, their custom of molong—claiming ownership of wild plants and trees in order to save them for later use—guided their management of natural resources.[5]

Other Isolated Hunter-Gatherer Tribes

East of Sarawak, in the Indonesian province of Irian Jaya (which shares its landmass with Papua New Guinea), live two hunter-gatherer tribes even more isolated than the Penan. The Korowai and Kombai were largely unfamiliar with Westerners until the 1970s, when they were befriended by Protestant missionaries who failed to convert them to Christianity.

The Korowai and Kombai, who are among 250 indigenous tribes living in Irian Jaya, lead nearly identical lives. They make their home in tree houses located as high as 150 feet in the air. They build the tree homes of sago palm fronds and share them with their hunting dogs and with domesticated pigs, which are reserved for dowries and for awards in the settlement of disputes. Tribespeople live high in the trees so as to keep an eye out for predators, hostile tribespeople, game animals, and sorcerers, the latter of which they greatly fear.

"The lives of [tribal members] are hard and their view of the world is spare," says *National Geographic* writer George Steinmetz, who contacted both tribes during the 1990s. "Humans live in the inner zone; the dead inhabit an outer zone. Beyond lies the great sea where all will perish as the world ends."[6]

The daily lives of the hunter-gatherer tribes, however, are concerned more with survival than philosophy. The forest in which they live is short on sizable game animals, so they must rely on birds, fish, even reptiles for daily meals. A prize kill is always the cassowary, a flightless and colorful Indonesian bird. Tribes will make use of the entire animal, including bones and feathers. Another staple of their diet is the innermost core of the sago palm, which is pulverized, moistened, and strained to make a dough. The women of the tribe also gather the grubs, or larvae, of the scarab beetle, which lays its eggs in the rotting centers of sago palm logs. In the Indonesian forest, nothing is wasted. And, as with the Penan, the rich culture of the Kombai and Korowai is closely tied to the animals and plants who also make their home within it.

Close to the Earth, Close to Each Other

Southeast Asia's indigenous tribespeople tie their livelihoods not only to the earth but also to each other. Within indigenous society the individual is not so important as the group: What is good for one must be good for all. Thus, over the centuries tribal societies created an entire culture based on the achievements of "the people," rather than the individual. Like most other societies on the earth, indigenous Southeast Asians have their cultural traditions: They conduct elaborate wedding ceremonies, create artwork and music unique to their society, wear distinctive clothing, and mourn their dead. But each of these art and cultural forms is an expression of the group as well as that of an individual artist or participant.

Chapter 2

The Family Circle

The notion of a nuclear family—mother, father, and children living together in one household—would be foreign to an indigenous tribal member who had never met a Westerner. Most tribal children grow up knowing their grandparents, aunts, uncles, and cousins intimately, since these relatives are involved in their care and upbringing. Most tribal members are related by blood in some way, though marriages are often arranged between members of different tribal groups—a tradition that probably developed as a way to build alliances and bring "new blood" into isolated villages.

Indigenous tribespeople know they must share their resources—food, housing, and so on—to survive. Because of this reality, they learn to put the group first, from the time they are born until the time they are old and preparing to die.

Childbirth Ceremonies

Like the members of every human society, Southeast Asian tribespeople gather to-

gether to welcome a newborn baby into their tribal family. Indigenous parents and their relatives usually have strict procedures they must follow, and if these procedures and conditions are met, they believe that both the baby and the tribe will know good health and good fortune. Nevertheless, the vulnerability of a newborn child is acknowledged, particularly with respect to evil spirits.

The Jeh, a Montagnard tribe, hold a ceremony that is meant to protect a new baby from the spirit world. When the baby is twelve days old, adult family members gather together and dip their fingers into a jar of rice wine. One by one, they pass their fingers across the mouth of the baby, and then the group kills a chicken as a spirit sacrifice.

This ceremony is meant to appease the spirit that lives in the house; it is known as the Kayh. The Jeh believe that a Kayh lives in each and every household and protects all the people that live there. Since the baby is a new member of the household, the Jeh offer a sacrifice and ceremony so that the Kayh will accept the baby and agree to protect it.

Naturally the adult members of any tribe offer what protection they can to a new infant; it is a responsibility they take very seriously. The Bajau, or Sea Gypsies, of the Philippines believe that certain actions they take after a baby's birth will affect the child's future for good or for ill. Immediately after a Bajau baby's birth, an adult member of the tribe, often a man, takes up the responsibility of gathering up the placenta, the membrane that surrounds the baby in the womb and is expelled during the birth process. He places the placenta in a coconut shell and takes it to the shoreline to bury it. While he is leaving the birthing place, members of the household engage in a time-honored ritual: They call to him while he is walking away. But no matter how often they call him, he must not look back. If he does, it is believed that the child, once grown, will always be looking over his shoulder.

A Gruesome Tradition

Not all tribal traditions associated with childbirth benefited the newborn. A writer who visited the Montagnard in 1968 recorded the story of a pregnant woman who had an unexpectedly difficult labor

A Vietnamese family gathers on their boat. Family connections are very important to the tribes of Southeast Asia.

while giving birth to her first child. Her husband did what he could: He built a fire to warm her and took her out of the house into the sunshine. He wrapped their healthy child in a blanket after it was born and massaged the mother's stomach, but to no avail. The woman died, though her child lived. According to village custom, the baby, living or not, would have to be buried with the mother, since there was no one else in the village to take care of it. The father hollowed out a log to make a coffin big enough for both mother and baby. An observer of the situation explained how he stepped in to save the baby's life: "I tried to convince someone to take the child, but the father did not want it and neither did the family," the observer reports. "I finally gave him [money] to let me send the child to a [clinic]. What are you going to do? It's the way they have lived for a thousand years."[7]

The tradition of infanticide probably developed during times when food was scarce and there were not enough nursing mothers in the tribe. Again, since the focus is always on the group, tribespeople probably felt that leaving the child with its deceased mother would be better for the tribe and its remaining children in the long run.

Family Life and Responsibilities

From the time they are able to stand and walk, indigenous children are expected to help contribute to the common good. Most of their early years are spent learning, though they do not attend school the way Western children do. Rather, they are taught life and work skills by the adults around them.

Tribes who survive by hunting and gathering pass these skills on to their children while they are very young. Boys in the Mentawai tribe of Indonesia learn how to carve an arrow as soon as they are able to hold a knife. From the age of four on, Mentawai boys practice shooting with bows and arrows. They each have their own small bows and quivers of arrows and use coconuts as targets. They graduate to hunting birds in the forest by the time they are seven. At the age of ten they will accompany the adult men on real hunts, learning how to find the animals by their scent and by the tracks they leave behind. Whether young or old, Mentawai tribesmen hunt with arrows dipped in poison made from a mixture of leaves, bark, and chiles, seeking out monkeys, deer, birds, frogs, and wild boar.

While they are still very young, Mentawai girls accompany their mothers and grandmothers to the local rivers to fish for freshwater shrimp and various kinds of fish. They will also go with them to gather plants and fruits from the jungle; by the time they are ten or older, the girls are usually going by themselves. In Mentawai society tasks are usually divided between the sexes; girls do not hunt and boys rarely gather.

For children of agrarian tribes, like the Hmong, childhood learning will focus on farming techniques and household chores. Both boys and girls will learn how to plant the fields and care for animals. But house-

Children are expected to help the tribe by working alongside adults. Here a group of Hmong women and children prepare for work.

hold chores are relegated to women only: Girls learn from their mothers how to cook corn, banana stalks, rice hulls, squash, and other foods for the daily meals. They will also learn how to embroider and make jewelry.

Despite all of the learning going on, life for tribal children is not all work and no play. A researcher who lived with the Mentawai in the 1990s describes children swimming in the rivers for the fun of it and rolling in the mud after a rain. In a Penan family, if the children are bored and one of the tribesmen has some spare time, he may entertain them with his blowpipe, the tool

used for hunting. He will use the pipe to blow nonpoisonous darts at various targets. The children will eagerly watch to see where the darts land and then bring them back for another round at the blowpipe.

And like children everywhere, the children who live in an indigenous tribe can always find a way to make work fun. When Kundstadter witnessed and recorded a swidden burn by a Karen tribe, he carefully noted the way the village children worked to turn their duties into a game: "The adults carefully watched the fire to make sure it didn't spread to the village, the children laughed happily as they worked to keep the flames back," he writes. In addition to helping their parents, the children also got a lesson about how to treat field spirits while a burn is going on, courtesy of the elders of the tribe: "Children joined in the fun, squirting the roofs with water guns made with bamboo cylinders . . . as the old ladies stood between their houses and the flames. They tossed salt from . . . trays as magic to make the wind blow away from the village."[8]

The Role of the Elderly

Tribal elders are revered by all for their knowledge and skill. Tribal lore and ex-

pertise is always passed along verbally or by example, and the elder members of the tribe, through their long years of experience, are often the teachers. The Bajau, for example, traditionally had great sailing skills that were passed along from generation to generation. Westerners who discovered them spoke in awe of how a Bajau sailor could dip his finger in the sea and tell how long it would take him to reach a destination, and of how he could give names to specific locations in the sea, just as land dwellers would name a mountain or mountain pass. No humans are born with such knowledge, of course; it must be taught by those who learned it from someone else. Thus, tribespeople like the Bajau have learned to prize life experience; it has helped them survive.

Tribespeople are expected to continue to contribute to the group, even as they age. But most tribes will take into consideration an aging member's frail body: An elderly woman, for example, will not be expected to accompany younger women on a fishing expedition. Instead, she will stay in the village and help mend torn nets. For hunter-gatherer tribes, mobility is crucial, but even they will make allowances for weaker members. The Penan, who move from place to place over a large area, will set up base camps where some members may stay for several weeks or

A boy poses with his grandfather, who is expected to pass on his knowledge and skills to younger generations.

months. "This base camp is for the very young and the very old," Eric Hansen wrote after visiting with a Penan tribe in the 1990s. Hansen also pointed out a truism that applies to other indigenous tribes besides the Penan: What Westerners think of as old—age seventy, eighty, or older— is rare in the indigenous world. "Forty is old for the Penan," Hansen says. "They age quickly because of the harsh environment and few live to reach fifty."[9]

Rules of Courtship

The customs of courtship in the indigenous world vary widely from tribe to tribe. Although tribal marriages are often arranged between families, the Hmong is one tribal group that allows its young people to choose their own mates. This usually occurs during the annual New Year festival. A boy or girl of that tribe is never chastised if he or she has a casual romance or flirtation before choosing a mate. However, once a choice is made, and an agreement between families reached, both partners are expected to remain faithful to one another.

The Hmong groom's family is expected to pay a dowry, or bride price, to the bride's family. Hmong families will often haggle and bargain before agreeing on a price, which is paid in silver, a metal much valued by the Hmong.

The paying of the bride price ties a Hmong woman to her husband's family even after his death. If he should die, then his eldest brother has the option of taking her as his wife. If she refuses to marry the brother and chooses someone else instead, she must return part of the bride price to her late husband's family.

The Bajau of Sarawak, the so-called cowboys of the East, pay their bride price not in silver, but in buffalo. Families who wish to win their son a wife from a good family must usually part with five or six head of buffalo along with other gifts. Buffalo is common as a bride price in other Malaysian tribes, though tribal members will also exchange heirloom jars, antique beads, and baskets as a way to win the mate of their choice.

Engagement and Wedding Ceremonies

When it comes to marriage, the Jarai of Vietnam allow their women to do the choosing. Once a woman makes her selection, a trusted intermediary will approach the man and his family. If they accept the third party's offer, then the couple is engaged to be married in a special ceremony. As both family and the intermediary look on, the couple exchanges bronze bracelets and promises to marry. As their wedding day approaches, both the man and the woman take care to remember the dreams they have each night so that others in the tribe can interpret them; it is believed that whatever dreams they have during this waiting period will foretell their life together.

Not all tribes host engagement ceremonies, but most will conduct elaborate wedding rituals, much like Westerners do. Such rituals can occupy an entire day and will, of course, get an entire village involved.

Wealth

Indigenous tribes do not have a monetary system based on coins or paper bills. They have always "purchased" items from each other, but used a barter system instead of money: A man who wanted another's tools might trade his pig or chickens for it.

The people do, however, have ways of measuring personal wealth, which is usually calculated by the number of prized possessions they own. Possessions of value vary from tribe to tribe: the Malaysian Bajau, the so-called cowboys of the East, are buffalo herders, and therefore measure their personal wealth by how many buffalo they own.

The Hmong prize silver above all else. The tribe has historically traded the opium they grow in their fields for bars of silver, which they then fashion into jewelry. Hmong jewelry—necklaces, earrings, and pendants—is beautifully crafted and often quite elaborate. Hmong families measure their wealth by this jewelry, all of which is worn openly by female members of the

tribe; thus, it is said that the Hmong wear their wealth around their necks.

One of the more unusual signs of wealth is found among the Yali, an Indonesian tribe. The Yali prize the cowrie shell, which is a shell of a species of mollusk. Like the Hmong, the Yali women will string their shells into a necklace and wear them proudly. But they are also not above using them as currency. If a Yali wants tobacco or a knife or weapon he cannot make himself, he will trade a few shells to get it.

As indigenous tribes are introduced more and more to the Western world, they have become accustomed to, and comfortable with, Western money. Many now hold Western-style jobs that come with a regular paycheck. And some, like the Hmong and the Karen of Thailand, will also sell their native jewelry and crafts for Western currency, which they will in turn use to buy Western clothes, food, radios, and televisions.

Yet among the seagoing Bajau, the bride and groom are not allowed to show happiness on their wedding day: Their emotions can be expressed only after the daylong festivities have ended. Before those festivities can begin, however, the bride must be prepared. She takes a ritual bath, then lets others take over. De Henning Singh, who witnessed a tribal wedding ceremony, provides details:

A shaman singles out a lock of her hair and blows on it three times, a charm to ensure well-being, and then pours seawater over her head. [The bride] winces as it trickles into her eyes. The wedding cosmetician uses a razor blade to trim her hair into bangs and shape her eyebrows into triangles . . . she is helped into a bright blue sarong with bold circular patterns. A curtain is drawn to conceal her. Now the groom . . . approaches. . . . He is carried on the shoulders of a friend. The curtain parts, [the bride's father] takes the groom's finger and guides it to his daughter's head and then to her breast. And so they are married.[10]

Polygamy and Trial Marriage

Once the wedding ceremony has ended, daily life must begin. Most brides will join their husband's family, although in a few areas of Southeast Asia, the couple will go to live in the bride's village instead.

Some tribes, like the Hmong, allow a woman to request a second wife in the household, so that she will have someone to help her keep house, take care of the children, pound rice, grind corn, and work in the fields. Even though the Hmong and the Karen insist on fidelity during marriage, they will allow a trial period for a young couple prior to the marriage being finalized. If the couple is not compatible, they are allowed to return to their respective families providing the bride price is repaid.

Elaborate wedding ceremonies are commonplace in Southeast Asia. Pictured is a bride and groom from the Kenyah Kayan tribe.

Polygamy is quite common in certain tribes, one in particular being the Kalinga of the Philippines, a tribe that is also known to engage in trial marriages. Kalinga men frequently have several wives and many children. This does not mean, however, that Kalinga wives operate as a democracy or even as a team. Each Kalinga family has an elder, or favorite wife, who makes most of the decisions and runs the household.

Native Crafts

Important as marriage and child rearing are in indigenous society, the need to create is also strong and has produced remarkable artifacts that are functional, decorative, or both. Almost every Southeast Asian tribe engages in handcrafts and carving of some sort. This native artwork is usually practical, having a real use in people's daily lives—a bowl to serve rice in, perhaps, or a canoe to be used in a special ceremony. Native artwork also reflects the tribe's strong ties to nature and to each other.

Hunter-gatherer tribes who live in Malaysia's forests usually carve their eating utensils so that they look like the animals they hunt or encounter in the jungle. The Ifuago of the Philippines, however, like to carve dinnerware that resembles a human being. The Ifuago spend so much time carving the spoons they use at mealtimes that they would often bring them along when they traveled. This was also considered a social courtesy: Since poorer tribes may not have extra spoons available

for their dinner guests, it is good manners to bring one's own.

Carving is usually left up to the men of the tribe while women expend their creative talents on their clothing. Hmong and Karen women are celebrated for their elaborate, handmade textiles.

The Hmong women also make paper goods, baskets, leather goods, and embroidery. The intricate hieroglyphic-like patterns on Hmong cloth is actually the remnant of an ancient written language. In the eighteenth century the Hmong were forbidden by Chinese authorities who then ruled in the area to use this language. Hmong mothers and daughters kept it alive for a time by incorporating its letters into textiles, but eventually the ability to use the language was lost. Now the ancient symbols are used only as decoration.

Music and Dance

Like people all over the world, indigenous tribespeople love to have a good time. And like their counterparts in the West and elsewhere in the world, having a good time usually involves music and dance. However, a tribal dance is rarely performed simply for the sake of dancing. It usually accompanies a special event, a religious spectacle, or the arrival of an honored guest.

The Iban tribe of Malaysia developed a dance in honor of one of its sacred animals, the hornbill, a bird that resembles a toucan. When the Iban want to honor the hornbill, they will weave replicas of the bird out of bamboo and colored clothes and hang them from tall poles in front of the tribes' longhouses. The men wear headdresses and arm ornaments made of hornbill feathers, and turn and swoop in imitation of the bird's flight. The hornbill dance is performed to the music of a native orchestra known as a gamelan. The gamelan is an instrument ensemble in which native musicians play drums, gongs, wooden xylophones, and metallophones, which look like xylophones but are made of metal instead of wood.

Not all tribal music must be accompanied by a dance. Many tribespeople love to sing whether they have a talent for music or not. The Bajau of the Philippines traditionally have a song for every occasion, and children, in particular, are encouraged to sing a made-up song about their situation if they are angry or upset. Such songs are known as *lia-lia,* and they are considered a safe way for children to vent their emotions. Bajau children are

The Kedang

The Kedang of Lembata, an island in southern Indonesia, have a complicated, formalized marriage ritual that some believe is symbolized by the remarkable *ikat adat,* an intricate, handmade cloth that is created by the woman in honor of her marriage. *Ikat adat* are made of cotton grown by the Kedang and woven and spun by their women. The cotton threads must be dyed before weaving begins, and the whole process can take years. Patterns vary from village to village and reflect the taste of the weaver herself. Once the *ikat adat* is completed, the woman's new family will keep it throughout her marriage.

The period that Westerners might refer to as the engagement begins with a family meeting, which must include certain relatives known as *mahan:* the man's maternal uncle's daughter and the woman's paternal's aunt's son, who are considered "al-

lies" of the prospective bride and groom. The groom's family must then give a series of gifts to the family of the bride. This gift-giving process has a series of stages, lasts years, and can sometimes go on after the couple has died; the marriage is not considered to be finalized until after all the gift giving has taken place. If either the husband or wife has indeed died, the children or grandchildren will finish the gift giving for them.

The bride's family receives the kinds of gifts highly valued in the Kedang community: bronze gongs and elephant tusks. The groom's family receives the *ikat adat* that the bride has woven. The Kedang believe that marriage is a ritual that cements two families together as well as two individuals. The long process of gift giving is meant to further strengthen the alliance between the two family groups.

A tribeswoman spins yarn, one of many crafts important to a tribe's well-being.

never punished for what they sing, even if the words are quite harsh.

Indigenous Music and a Western Reaction

When Westerners first began to explore Southeast Asia and encountered native tribes, the tribespeople were usually quite friendly and treated their visitors like honored guests. Their welcome usually included a performance by tribal musicians and artists, and the reaction could be quite mixed, even in the early twentieth century when visits to indigenous homelands had become more common.

Dean C. Worcester, the American secretary of the interior of the Philippines, became acquainted with tribal customs in the early 1900s, and his initial reaction was less than appreciative: "[The people] love music and dancing," he wrote. "They indulge in a monotonous crooning, varied with loud shrieks. . . . For hours at a time they keep up a monotonous circle dance each performer having his forefinger hooked into the waistband of the skirt or clout of the person in front of him."[11]

Not all Westerners felt as Worcester did, though. A group of British adventurers who visited with the Iban people during the nineteenth century would later describe a dance performed by the women in their honor to be a thing of beauty and more:

It was slow, undulating, seductive, tender. As the dancers stood motionless before us, their draperies hung straight from their chins to their toes, their feet being hidden in the folds of their petticoats. When they slowly lifted their arms, an undulation wrinkled up the folds of their garments as though a sigh, beginning at their heels, ran upwards and lost itself in the air above their heads.[12]

Festivals and Festival Customs

Some indigenous customs and celebrations seem to have been established, at least in part, so that the tribe can enjoy some of its favorite foods. Just as American families love to eat turkey on Thanksgiving, the Korowai and Kombai tribes of Indonesia make a party out of eating the grubs, or larvae, that hatch in the rotted logs of the Indonesian sago palm.

Tribespeople prepare a place for the grubs to grow by carefully cutting, splitting, and tying palm logs. They are then left to rot so the beetles can enter to lay their eggs. After two months, the eggs hatch and the grubs are collected for roasting and eating. The feast itself includes chanting and dancing, often continuing through the night. Korowai and Kombai women want to look their best for the festivities, so they take extra care, shaving their heads bald with a razor of split bamboo.

The rationale for such customs as eating grubs and shaving women's heads can be difficult for a Westerner to understand. However, many familiar Western customs simply have no place in indigenous society and would seem equally incomprehensible to any tribe who witnessed them. Journalist Stan Sesser, who visited with

Musicians play wooden xylophones, a traditional instrument, during an important festival.

The Drums of Vietnam

Metalsmiths on the mainland of Southeast Asia began working in bronze sometime between 2000 and 500 B.C. and may have learned to do so through their contact with the Chinese. Bronze was a much-prized metal, highly coveted by people of wealth and power. Most metalsmiths were eager to work in it, but those smiths who worked in a location known as Dongson, situated in the Thanh Hoa province of northern Vietnam, created a particularly lasting bronze artifact.

Measuring as high as three feet and weighing as much as 220 pounds, Dongson drums were used both as musical instruments and as cult objects. They were etched with intricate geometric patterns and designs that featured scenes of daily life and warfare as well as animals and birds.

Dongson drums became such coveted art objects that royalty often owned them. Whenever an army invaded an enemy kingdom, any Dongson drums in the royal court would be seized and taken home as booty.

Dongsons play an important part in Southeast Asia's archaeological history; they are widespread in the region, proving, researchers say, that early peoples moved about freely in their world and engaged in trade with one another. Dongson drums, they say, appear to have been used in trade agreements. More than two hundred drums were made in Southeast Asia, as far east as Indonesia and as far north as southern China. Archaeological remains on the Pasemah Plateau of South Sumatra, Indonesia, depict a man carrying a Dongson drum.

the Kayan of Sarawak while he researched a book, attended a Kayan party where he was warmly received and fed rice wine. Nonetheless, he still felt the gulf between East and West as the party came to an end. "Kayan gatherings end in a way that Westerners find strange," he said. "Anyone ready to leave simply gets up and walks out, without so much as a nod; there isn't a word for 'goodbye' in the Kayan language."[13]

The Road to War

Indigenous tribespeople throughout the region have nurtured a rich and varied culture that stretches back through generations. However, for that culture and its accompanying family life to survive, a political system had to be put in place to keep tribal society stable. This meant that the tribes had to choose leaders, form a tribal government, and in some cases, go to war against their neighbors.

Chapter 3

Lances and Longhouses

In today's world, tribal government plays a much smaller role than ever before. Many indigenous groups must now deal with provincial and national government officials instead of just their local chiefs and elders. National government officials have also discouraged local rule in an effort to promote national, rather than tribal, unity. For example, the center of most tribal governments is the longhouse. The tribal chief and his council, as well as some of the elders, use the longhouse as a meeting place in which to discuss issues and problems, and to make decisions. Governments, particularly in Indonesia, have discouraged the building of longhouses, preferring that Western-style homes be built instead. However, the longhouse has made somewhat of a comeback in some villages where tribespeople continue to look to their own leaders to secure their futures.

As with everything else in indigenous life, tribal leadership and decision making revolves around what is good for the group. However, the decision making itself tends not to be democratic—individuals considered to be in positions of authority will make the decisions for the group. In other words, the group informally delegates to a select number of individuals the power to make decisions affecting everyone.

Leaders and Decision Making

Most tribal villages have a head chief. In many villages the chief also has a council of tribal elders to confer with when making his or her decisions. Most tribal chiefs are male, but there are some notable exceptions. The Ra De, a Montagnard tribe, live under a matriarchal system whereby an elder woman in the group is tribal leader, or a *khao sang* in their language. The *khao sang* oversees community affairs and settles personal disputes. She is also the keeper of family heirlooms, which usually included bronze gongs, the ancient jars used for preparing rice beer, and the special stools that are used by musicians and party hosts. The *khao sang* even dispenses her decisions from a kind of throne—a seat carved from a single tree trunk; something that only the *khao sang* is allowed to use.

Sometimes a chief is chosen because of his or her age or brave deeds, but in some cases, personal qualities are taken into consideration. When Anne De Henning Singh visited with Bajau tribespeople in the Philippines, she spent time with their leader, a man named Sarani. The Bajau called him their "wise man" and he had been given his place of honor for several reasons: He could speak Filipino as well as their tribal language, and had served in the Philippine air force. Sarani was also the only member of that seagoing group who owned a motorized boat.

The kinds of disputes tribal leaders will settle, and the decisions they will make, range from mundane to life threatening. Two tribesmen quarrel over a herd of livestock and go before the chief to decide who really owns it. A seagoing tribe like the Bajau has bad luck fishing for weeks on end; the tribe's chief is the one to decide that the group will pull up anchor and try its luck elsewhere. Or, in extreme cases, if there is a dispute with another tribe or village, the chief and the tribal council are the ones who decide whether to go to war.

The Tools of War

Warriors of every tribe put a great deal of time and care into their weapons. Today,

Tribal elders use a longhouse as a meeting place to make important decisions.

these deadly tools are considered works of art and are sold in Western art galleries and to individual collectors. The kinds of weapons used varied a good deal from tribe to tribe. The Kalinga favored slender but deadly axes and lances. The Dyak of Indonesia carried spears, blowpipes, and machete-like swords that were known as *mandaus.*

Ifuago warriors lashed wooden boards together with rattan and used them as shields in battle. In the Filipino tribe known as the Bukidnon, warriors even put together a kind of body armor. Before a battle, they would wrap themselves in a native material known as kapok, or tree cotton, and tie the kapok in place with strips of cloth.

The Bukidnon became legendary among some Westerners for the way they would greet visitors to their village. As the visitors approached, the Bukidnon would send out a fully armed warrior. He would carry a long lance with a bell on the end of its handle. He would dance in front of them in a formal display of aggression— making faces, thrusting out his tongue, and shaking his lance as though he planned to use it. The Bukidnon warrior did not necessarily mean these visitors harm; however, they would know that this village was well protected from harm.

But this Bukidnon warrior did a lot more than just let the outsiders know his village was well protected. He made a scene to show off—letting them know how strong and powerful he is. Warriors spend a good deal of time showing off to their families, to outsiders, and to each other.

This is because the best warriors are also considered to be the best men. And in many respects, they are: Only the strongest and most able-bodied are allowed to go along on raids. Because they are so healthy and strong, they are considered prime catches for the young women of the tribe; a great warrior will have no trouble finding a mate to bear his children. Hence, there is much incentive for a young man to become a warrior, whether he is a member of the Bukidnon tribe or not.

The Reasons for War

Significantly, even the most warlike of tribes did not fight for the sake of fighting. Most battles were over food, women, or territory. Something as simple as a theft might set things off: If one tribe made off with another's herd of goats (or maybe the chief's daughter), the victims would want to seek revenge. Indeed, many battles were inspired by the need to right a wrong.

The Asmat of Indonesia, once known as fierce warriors, are today celebrated for their elaborate and beautiful "ancestor" poles. These ancestor poles, though, held a rather deadly purpose in the Asmat warrior culture. The artist would carve the faces of ancestors who had been killed by an enemy so that he would remember which of his relatives he had to avenge. This need for vengeance could fuel cycles of violence that lasted for years: One tribe would attack and kill so as to avenge the deaths of its members. The victims would then be obligated to do a retaliatory raid to avenge *their* dead.

Indonesian tribesmen perform a ceremonial dance to celebrate victory in battle.

Strategies Planned, Victory Celebrated

Indigenous tribesmen do not go to war in the Western sense. Instead of meeting in a pitched battle on an open field, warriors were more likely to hide along a jungle trail and ambush their enemies while they went about their business. Or the tribe conducted raids on a village when its inhabitants least expected it.

When a raid was successful, the winners brought trophies home with them—usually decapitated heads. Once arriving home they held a victory party. When an Ifuago war party returned from a successful raid, they arrived at the village in a sort of parade formation. Bent low to the ground, carrying steelheaded lances and shields, they beat their shields with sticks of wood. As they moved, posturing and making noise, they swayed in unison, left to right.

During their victory celebration, the Kalinga allowed the hero of the battle his moment in the spotlight. Once this celebration was under way, the star warrior stepped into the circle of onlookers. Like a famous quarterback describing the winning Super Bowl play, he would tell them the story of how he persevered in battle. Worcester, who traveled among the Philippine tribes, witnessed such occasions and described one in detail:

> Into the [circle] steps the hero of the occasion, dressed in his best clothes, decked with his gaudiest ornaments, bearing the shield, lance, and head-axe used in the recent fight. With word and gesture he describes his recent exploit. . . . After concluding his pantomimic discussion of his [exploit] he describes and boasts of previous achievements.[14]

Cannibalism

Primitive tribes like the Yali and Asmat have historically eaten their enemies, believing that this allowed them to absorb a dead warrior's strength and spirit. The Asmat, in particular, ate the brains of their captives, believing this was the best way to tap into the warrior's strength and power.

Decapitated heads of enemies taken as trophies were usually not eaten. Some tribes even made the heads a part of the victory celebration that took place later on. They would place the head on a bamboo pole in the open, and a tribal member, usually an elder, would berate the head for the sins of its village, and explain to it why it was taken from its owner's body.

The Naga of Myanmar are one of several tribes who "divide" up the head among the war party. Each warrior cuts away a piece of the head and takes it home with him as a trophy. Whatever remains of the head is left atop the village's ceremonial drum, which is shaped like a hornbill.

Montagnard Proxy Warriors

Although most tribal disputes arise over land, people, or resources, sometimes the kind of simmering hatred that lasts for generations can overtake an indigenous population. The Montagnard tribes, long disliked by their lowland neighbors, have suffered from such hatred for many years.

Colonial powers in Southeast Asia took advantage of the rivalry between the lowlanders and the Montagnards, using the latter as proxy warriors during the Cold War in the latter half of the twentieth century. The Cold War marked a period of tension between the United States (and its democratic allies) and the Soviet Union (and its Communist allies). The Cold War began at the end of World War II and lasted for nearly fifty years, punctuated by shooting wars in Korea and Vietnam. The French, who ruled Vietnam for nearly a century beginning in 1854, had allowed the Montagnards to live independently in their traditional highland homelands. But when France withdrew their forces in the 1950s, the new Vietnamese government abolished Montagnard independence, relocated lowland Vietnamese onto Montagnard lands, and forced Montagnard children to learn

Headhunting

Headhunting was an ancient and widespread practice among the indigenous tribes of Southeast Asia, particularly if they were hunter-gatherers and lived on the island nations of Indonesia, Malaysia, and the Philippines. Headhunting became much more rare and secretive after Western colonists arrived, since those governments strongly condemned the practice.

An enemy's head—as opposed to other parts of his body—was taken in battle because it was believed that the spirit of the slain man would be at the service of whoever possessed his head; this of course increased the victor's own power as a warrior.

The process of preserving a captured head varied somewhat from tribe to tribe. Some tribes would simply smoke their grisly souvenir over a fire, dry it out, and then hang it up in the longhouse. The Bontoc held much more elaborate rituals: Once the victory feast had ended, the head would be taken down from its place of honor and boiled in water to clean it. The lower jaw was then removed and the skull buried in a special room. After a year it would be dug up again and hung in a basket from the ridgepoles of the longhouse. The Ifuago also boiled heads, but did not bury them. Instead, the warrior who took the head would bring it home, taking care to fasten the lower jaw in place with rattan so it would not become dislodged. Many Ifuago households used heads taken in battle as decorations.

A warrior who lost his head in battle was considered a disgrace to his family. His headless body would be taken for burial far from his village. A lance would be thrust in the ground to show that he was killed in battle. Dean C. Worcester, America's secretary of the interior of the Philippines, told of attending one Ifuago funeral in which the deceased was berated by his family for being foolish enough to get killed.

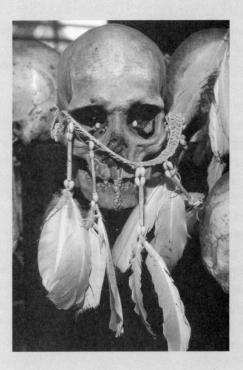

Headhunting, an ancient practice, often involved keeping skulls as a symbol of victory.

Vietnamese. Not surprisingly, a resistance movement brewed, and in 1964, the Montagnards led an armed revolt against their Vietnamese masters.

Though the revolt was unsuccessful the Montagnards would get a reprieve from the United States. The Vietnam conflict was heating up, and the Montagnards were being wooed by both sides: the South Vietnamese and America, and the Vietcong, or North Vietnamese Communists backed by China. The Montagnards soon abandoned any thoughts of an alliance with the Vietcong, however. An American army sergeant learned why when he visited a Montagnard village in 1968:

A Montagnard soldier in the central highlands of South Vietnam. Because uniforms were not standard issue, some Montagnard soldiers wore loincloths.

When the Vietcong first came here, they made all kinds of promises, saying that the revolution would bring autonomy [self-rule] to those who support it. The next time they took things. They gradually took control of all the poultry, the pigs, the eggs . . . they drafted youths, used villagers as [servants] for supply. . . . This was the cause of the suffering and separation of families.[15]

The Montagnards had cast their lot with the United States, and with their old enemy, the South Vietnamese government. In return, South Vietnam restored many of the Montagnard institutions it had outlawed.

Montagnard warriors quickly gained a reputation as brave and loyal fighters admired by their American counterparts. In 1969, First Lieutenant Roy C. Russell wrote optimistically of the Montagnards' chances for a bright future and for self-rule: "[The Montagnards] know this is the 20th century and that it is time they have a place in the future of the country. It is doubtful they will let anyone forget [them]."[16]

Russell's optimism for his Montagnard comrades proved misplaced, however. After the U.S. pullout from Vietnam in 1973, the Montagnards' interests took second place as the South Vietnamese government fought for survival. Montagnard villages were abandoned and its people resettled elsewhere, living in squalid conditions. Even before the final victory by the Vietcong, Vietnam's Montagnards had become a tribe of refugees.

Proxy Warriors Among the Hmong of Laos

Laos's Hmong were yet another highland tribe disliked by its lowland neighbors and friendly with the French, who had colonized part of the Indochina peninsula in addition to Vietnam. And like their counterparts, the Montagnards, the Hmong were later left to their own devices because the Westerners withdrew from their country. In 1953, Vietnamese Communists invaded northern Laos, where the Hmong lived. Laos had its own force of Communist fighters, a nationalist group known as the Pathet Lao, and some Hmong did join them; however, most were loyal to the pro-Western royal Lao government. In 1955, officials from America's Central Intelligence Agency (CIA) arrived to train eager Hmong, who would serve U.S. interests as indigenous fighting forces against communism: "The Hmong . . . were ready recruits for the CIA's secret army," says journalist Stan Sesser. "Young men who had never seen a car or an electric light were plucked

from primitive villages and put into jet fighters and helicopter gunships."[17]

The Hmong fought a secret war alongside the Americans in Laos for years, and like the Montagnards adjusted well to modern weaponry and Western fighting techniques. They also put their knowledge of the local terrain to good use. Scholar and journalist Jane Hamilton-Merritt, who reported from Laos and actually lived with the Hmong in their refugee camps, describes the widening of this secret war in the 1960s, and the diligence and courage of the Hmong. She quotes the words of a Hmong soldier, who was telling her of his dangerous duties alongside the American forces who fought in Laos:

> Many Hmong died trying to rescue the American pilots who were shot down. Often the communists had already captured the pilots or killed them. So, the communists hid their positions waiting for [our] soldiers to come to the area. They knew we would come and then they could kill us. Many Hmong died like this, trying to save the Americans.[18]

The United States finally acknowledged the war in Laos in 1970. But in the meantime, thousands of Hmong had died, and many more had been driven into the lowland jungles of Laos, far away from their mountain homes. When the Pathet Lao took over the country in 1975, the Hmong's leader, Vang Pao, fled to Thailand. Thousands of Hmong ended up fleeing Laos, and more than a hundred thousand Hmong refugees made their way to the United States.

The Dyak of Indonesia

Indonesia was largely untouched by the Cold War, but the country's efforts to stem overpopulation problems and rampant poverty in the last decade touched off a long-lasting tribal dispute that at times grew shockingly violent. After the territory of West Kalimantan became a separate Indonesian province, the government encouraged the Madurese, a Muslim people, to resettle themselves in what had historically been Dyak land. The Dyak, who are largely Christian, tried to drive out the Madurese during the 1990s. Observers reported that this particular conflict was over both land and religion. And the two combatants, they say, were like oil and fire together. In 1997 fighting became so heated that the Indonesian army had to step in. Australian journalist Patrick Walters spoke to local residents who said that ancient Dyak warrior techniques had made a comeback during this conflict: "Catholic priests tell of hundreds of Madurese being killed, many of them decapitated in accordance with traditional Dyak rituals and their hearts and livers being cut out and eaten."[19]

An angry Dyak youth in front of a burning Madurese house.

These same Dyaks, Walters was told, called upon their ancient rites to prepare for battle: They performed a ceremony known as *teriu,* whereby warriors assumed a trance-like state and called for the blessings of their ancestral spirits and gods of the forest.

Peaceful Penan

No discussion of war and government among the often war-oriented peoples of Southeast Asia can be complete without citing a counterexample: the Penan, one of the most peaceful tribes in the region. Penan have little hierarchy and make almost all their decisions as a group. They have almost no history of violence. Researcher Bruno Manser, who spent years living with the Penan, said they put cooperation above all else: "There was a boy in the [Penan] group who caught seven fish," he said. "I remember watching the headman give three to each family and then carefully slice the remaining fish in two. This is the Penan. You will never find one with a full stomach and another hungry."[20]

The Penan almost never quarrel. Manser said only once did he see a hungry child neglect to share food. Writer Eric Hansen, who walked across Borneo in 1982, was another outsider who came away with lasting impressions of the Penan. He remembered asking what would be a serious crime in the Penan community: "[The tribesmen] conversed for a minute, as though they were having difficulty thinking of any crime," Hansen says. "Then [one of the men] explained the concept of see-hun, which means to be stingy or not to share."[21]

The Penan are a nomadic community, but there is an affinity between tribal groups who may rarely encounter each other. As Penan wander the forest, they leave signs for each other—signs made of wooden sticks to show each other who is going where, and why.

Violence Balanced with Spirituality

Although conflict is second nature to many indigenous tribes, spirituality is also important in their culture. Every tribe studied by modern researchers has a belief system corresponding to a religion as the term is understood by Westerners. Most tribes believe in a creator who made the world and everything in it. However, they also believe the creator has little to do with day-to-day life. That role is filled by the spirit world, which the tribes must learn to appease and live with properly if they are to prosper in this world.

Chapter 4

Nature Has a Soul

In the indigenous belief system, all things—plants, animals, weapons, ornaments, and even stones—have a spirit living inside of them. These spirits can do evil or good, and tribespeople must live their lives in ways that will not disturb or anger them. If a spirit is angry with a person, it could make the person sick. But if the spirits are appeased and happy, they will ensure that the year's rice crop is a good one.

Most tribes rely on holy men or women known as shamans to help people communicate with the spirit world. Such shamans employ a number of tools, such as spirit-friendly charms and talismans, to facilitate that communication. When dealing with the spirits, the sacrifice of animals and exorcism—the casting out of bad spirits—were common practices until relatively recently, but still occur in remote, rural areas or in thinly populated mountain regions.

Placating the Spirits with Animal Sacrifice and Rituals

Some tribes believe that spirits "take sides"—that some are good and some are bad, and one must know the difference. The Melanau, a fishing tribe that lives along the coast of Sarawak, calls the good spirits *tou,* and the bad, belum: If encountered, the *belum* will cause humans sickness and trouble. But the *tou* are considered more powerful than the *belum,* a belief that may account for the Melanau's relatively sunny outlook on life.

Other tribes believe that any spirit can do harm if it is provoked—and it can be quite easy to provoke a spirit. The Hmong believe that if one conducts one's self improperly on a journey, the spirit of the trail will be angered. And if the spirit is angered, the traveler will fall on the trail and sprain an ankle. According to another belief, if one crosses the threshold of a Hmong home and bangs one's head on the doorway, the spirit who lives in the house will be angered. Bad luck will follow the offender everywhere, the Hmong believe, until the person sacrifices an animal to the spirit and mounts the animal's legs over the doorway as a goodwill gesture.

Two Indonesian shamans, the spiritual leaders of a tribe, pose in traditional dress.

Failure to placate an angry spirit can be blamed for bringing disaster to a village. In one Hmong village in the 1970s, several residents had died mysteriously and unexpectedly. Upon deciding that the spirit of a certain rock had been offended by crops that had been planted nearby, the people concluded that the spirit had cursed the village. Thus they removed all the plants near the rock and watched the local shaman sacrifice a pig to the spirit. After smearing the rock with pig blood, he performed rituals meant to placate the rock's spirit. The Western journalist who reported this incident did not remain in the village to see whether the mysterious deaths stopped.

The Shaman's Role

Other than the chief or the tribal elders, the shaman is the most important person in the tribe. Part doctor, part priest, and part mystic, the shaman communicates with the spirits, asks for their goodwill, and begs their pardon for any offenses the tribe may have committed. The main criterion for being a shaman is the ability to communicate effectively with the spirits. Effectiveness, in turn, is measured in terms of cures for illness attributed to the shaman and evidence that the spirits have forgiven the people for offenses.

The Bidayuh, a people who live in the hilly interior of western Sarawak, Malaysia, have female shamans. These women run the spiritual life of the tribe and wear tall, beaded, conical hats, which identify them, no less than the distinctive vestments or robes of Western clergy or Eastern monks.

But the Mentawai shamans, called *sikeireis,* are men, and the villages of this Indonesian tribe tend to have more than one. *Sikeireis* work as a team, since a group effort is considered more powerful.

When contacting the spirits, *sikeireis* usually share a ritual meal of domestic pig or wild boar first. They then speak a series of magic chants and do a ritual dance, after which they enter into a trance during which the spirits "speak" to them.

Spirits That Heal or Hurt

A shaman must do more than speak with the spirits. Since most tribes believe sickness is caused by the spirit world, the shaman is also the tribal doctor. The Hmong believe that when a person gets sick, the person's soul has somehow left the body. The tribal shaman, known by

The Complicated Cosmology of the Naga

Most indigenous tribes believe in an underworld, but the Naga, who live in Myanmar along the region that borders Assam, have a complicated view of the universe that involves a land of the dead *and* a world of heavenly creatures.

The Naga believe that when people die, they go to a land that is under the world where the living resides. The bottom of the Naga's world is the "sky" of the underworld, and whenever night comes, it is daytime in this underworld. Good people are rich and happy in this underworld, and evil people are poor and miserable, they believe. The Naga also believe they can maintain a relationship with the underworld by collecting round stones, which symbolize the earth. The stones, which are prized by the Naga, are kept in the communal men's house and in the granaries, in hopes they will encourage a good harvest.

Far more powerful in the minds of the Naga than the residents of the underworld are the Potso, or sky people. The Naga believe that the sky over their heads serves as a floor for the world of the Potso. In return, the Potso have a sky over their head, and it in turn serves as a floor for yet another world of sky people. These "worlds" go on indefinitely, like endless layers of "parallel universes."

A shaman (far right) performs a ceremony that includes offerings of wild boar to powerful spirits.

them as the *tu-ua-neng,* must lure the soul back into the patient's body—something he will accomplish by chanting and jangling noisemakers, in addition to other rituals he may perform.

The Karen have an opposite belief: They believe that sickness is caused by an invading spirit. To heal the patient, the Karen shaman places a food offering between himself and a sick person; this will entice the invading spirit to leave the body, he believes. The shaman then urges the spirit into a basket, which will be taken into the woods so that the spirit can be sent on its way. Then, a few sym-

bolic thorny plants are placed on the porch ladder leading up to the doorway of the house to prevent the spirit from returning.

The Penan are another tribe that believes spirits infect the sick person. But their shaman has a different technique: He entices the spirit onto a raft. He sets the raft adrift to float down the river so the trapped spirit cannot harm the tribe again.

For the seagoing Bajau tribe, the patient's participation can be as important as that of the shaman. Anne De Henning Singh, who witnessed a Bajau cure that required the patient to interact with a neighbor he had offended, describes a dramatic scene:

> The drums beat rhythmically as the sick man lay under a green cloth, his eyes shiny with fever. . . . Suddenly, with a loud shriek, he jumps up and leaps from one boat to another. Dressed in green and white, the colors of the spirits, he flings his arms in the air and tramples the deck furiously. The gongs go wild. Now a second man, dressed like the first, leaps from another [boat], joins in the same convulsion, and utters an incomprehensible stream of words—the language of the spirits.[22]

As the ceremony continued, onlookers laughed and threw talcum powder on the two men to "revive" them. Afterward, the two men rose, kissed, and shook hands. One of the tribesmen told De Henning Singh that the sick man had fallen ill because he had wronged the other man. He further explained that the spirits, angered by the quarrel, had cursed the instigator with a fever.

Shamans Who Use Healing Plants

In addition to communicating with spirits, healers use a knowledge of the natural world. Indeed, many are well versed in the healing properties of native plants. The plants Mentawai put in their charms are all known to have medicinal qualities. A plant called *daun parencis* will heal a nasty cut.

Aromatic leaves will reduce the pain of sore joints, and the roots of certain plants relieve the toxicity of scorpion and snake bites.

Writer Jean-Philippe Soulé, who lived for a time with the Mentawai, witnessed the preparation of talismans for a dangerous jungle journey:

> The sikeireis collected . . . medicinal plants and roots, which they placed on the base of a sago leaf. On the [leaf] were put little pieces of the root of the requisite [special plants. . . . Some small white chicken feathers were trimmed into a narrow band of very clean leather. Those were added to the one end of the [leaf]. Everything was wrapped in pieces of narrow fabric.[23]

Small ropes were affixed to the completed bundles, to enable the people to wear the charms around their necks. A newborn baby, needing the most protection, wore the largest talisman of all.

Harvest Rituals

Since farming is so important in Southeast Asia, tribespeople take care not to anger spirits that live in the fields. The Karen have a complicated ritual for planting and harvest. When a field is weeded for the first time, they will cry out, "Rice, O! Come back good again. Return white again. Come back thick and swaying dark. Come back green and spreading. Return and fill last year's field."[24]

Later on in the year, when the rice is ready to be harvested, the spirits must be notified to protect the valuable crop from

Shamans give thanks for the year's crops by performing harvest rituals.

thieves. Each night tribespeople come out to mark their rice with twisted straw or woven bamboo to let the spirits know that rice belongs to them and must not be stolen. They also offer a new chant asking the spirits for their goodwill next year: "Proo! Rice soul. Return to the top of the rice fields. Come back inside the rice field. . . . Return to fill the fields and granaries."[25]

The Mnong, a Montagnard tribe, hold sacrifices for the harvest in four phases. One ritual must be completed before the land is cleared, another before the seed is planted, a third when the rice is half grown, and a fourth after the harvest. Vil-

lagers sacrifice a cow for the third phase, leading it to the rice field and accompanied by the shaman. The children of the village go with him, and they are followed by six musicians carrying huge gongs. Small bits of skin are cut from the cow's ear and buried along the borders of the rice field. A huge decorative pole is placed in a clearing near the village, and offerings of rice, bananas, and eggs are placed under the pole. The musicians and shaman circle the pole and chant: "We live here with good water, with good fields, in fine house. We thank you for the last harvest, and we ask you for a new harvest. Don't let the rain destroy us. Don't let the lightning come."[26]

After the prayer is finished, the village executioner kills the cow with a ceremonial ax. The sacrificed cow is then butchered, and an equal share of meat goes to each family.

The Living and the Dead

In indigenous society, the dead are very much a part of everyday life. The Bidayuh remember their dead by carving figures of them from wood. These figures are placed along the footpaths leading to the villages and longhouses. As long as they are there,

the people will be protected, the Bidayuh believe.

The Asmat, who live in swampy areas of Indonesia, give water a major role in their belief systems. They believe that the water's surface divides the world of those who live above the water and those who live beneath; hence there are two worlds, one above the water and one below. Counterparts of the living can be seen in their reflections in the water, and that place beneath the surface is also a world of the dead, where their ancestors live. In Asmat carvings, the people are often facing one another, limbs entwined and

Wooden effigies in rememberance of the dead are displayed on rocky ledges in many of Southeast Asia's indigenous societies.

Mummies of the Philippines

The Ibaloi are Filipino tribespeople who mummify their dead, an uncommon practice among the primitive tribes of Southeast Asia. It is believed that the Ibaloi began embalming wealthier members of their tribe sometime in the eleventh century. Ideally, the embalming process began before death when a person on the point of dying would drink saltwater to cleanse his or her organs. After death, the body would be washed and rubbed with herbs, then alternately dried in the sun and cured over a slow-burning fire. The body would then be wrapped in blankets and laid to rest in a cave that served as a family burial plot.

Much like the ancient Egyptians, the Ibaloi embalmed their dead to prepare them for the afterlife. But unlike the Egyptians, they did not remove the body's internal organs, meaning that their mummies are not nearly as well preserved as those found in Egypt. After the arrival of the Spaniards in the 1500s, the practice of embalming went into decline. Some long-hidden mummies were discovered in the twentieth century, thus provoking the interest of tourists. About fifty Ibaloi mummies were stolen before the government stepped in. In 1999, one of the stolen mummies, a war king by the name of Apo Annu, was returned to his resting place.

In 2000, Filipino officials stepped up security and allowed teams of scientists to examine the mummies. The Ibaloi remain very respectful of their dead, however, refusing to reveal the location of the mummies that still remain hidden. When scientists ask to see mummies that have already been located, the Ibaloi perform animal sacrifices and prayer rituals prior to allowing any examinations to take place.

The Ibaloi believe that whoever moves a mummy from its resting place will be cursed. So far scientists have examined and returned the mummies without dramatic consequences, except perhaps for one man, who reported falling down a slope and fracturing his ribs after cracking a joke during an Ibaloi ritual.

A tribesman poses with an Ibaloi mummy, rarely displayed to outsiders.

looking distorted and wavy, like reflections in water. The Asmat ceremonial canoe, or soul ship, has no bottom so that the water's surface can be seen while it is floating. The canoe is intricately carved with figures who perch on the gunwales and lean over the water, hoping to see their ancestors there.

Death Rituals

Because of the people's belief in an afterlife, indigenous funeral rituals tend to be quite elaborate. The Murut of Indonesia mourn their dead in an elaborate ritual that goes on for several days. On the day after death, the corpse is arranged in a fetal position and placed in a large earthen jar, along with some personal belongings. The mouth of the jar is closed, then placed on a special platform for a time. Later, the jar becomes a coffin, buried in the earth. Over the grave the Murut build a hut that they paint, decorate, and fill with additional belongings of the dead person.

In the seagoing Bajau culture, the corpses are washed, dressed, kept in a boat overnight, then taken to a nearby island that the tribe reserves for burials. A carving, usually of a motorized boat, is placed over the dead person's face. This reflects the belief that life will go on in the next world, and therefore a boat will be needed for transportation. With the arrival of Western culture, motorized boats became particularly coveted, though few Bajau obtain one in their lifetimes.

These complicated death rituals are based on a belief that the dead live again

in another world, one unseen by the living. Primitive tribes did not believe that a dead person would actually come back and live again in their world; this changed, however, when they were introduced to the religions of India and China, some of which include a belief in reincarnation.

Eastern Religion

The Indian traders and Chinese conquerors who came from the east and south, respectively, in the early part of the first millennium brought their religious beliefs with them. In many respects these were the most important things they left behind. Hinduism, Buddhism, Confucianism, and later Islam, which originated in the Mideast, had a deep and lasting impact on most of Southeast Asia, including the more remote and reclusive hill tribes. The Hmong of Vietnam, for example, were among those tribes who gained a belief in reincarnation because of their exposure to imported religious beliefs, Buddhism in particular.

Those Vietnamese tribespeople who converted to Buddhism keep a *chua,* or pagoda, in their village center even today. A statue of the Buddha is kept there, and on the first and fifteenth days of the month, villagers visit the Buddha, bringing him flowers and fruit as gifts.

Until the thirteenth century, Hinduism held tremendous influence in the region as the kings and ruling classes of Southeast Asia sought to import not only India's national religion, but also its ideas of kingship, court ritual, literature, and fine arts.

Even today, cultural institutions that originated in India are still practiced in the region, including shadow puppet theater—the characters are cutouts that cast a shadow on a screen when manipulated by a puppeteer.

But Hinduism's influence on the region waned after the thirteenth century as India began to pass into Muslim hands. Based on the teachings of the prophet Muhammad, the Muslim faith, first carried eastward by Arab traders, created massive conversions in Southeast Asia throughout the fifteenth and sixteenth centuries. Today, Islam is the dominant religion of the people of Malaysia, Brunei, Indonesia, and the southern Philippines.

However, the region's indigenous tribespeople rarely converted wholeheartedly to any outside faith. Rather, they tended to integrate the ideas of others into their traditional beliefs about the spirit world. Hence, a tribesman who was a Buddhist also took care to listen to his shaman to avoid angering the spirits.

The Arrival of Christianity

Christianity, too, had a deep impact on Southeast Asia's culture and spirituality—but had much less success than either Buddhism or Islam. This is mostly because of the attitudes of the European Christians who first came to the region. Examples of European offensiveness and insensitivity toward the native populations are extremely numerous. D.R. Sardesai, author of *Southeast Asia, Past and Present*, and a scholar who has made Southeast Asian history his life's work, writes of the trouble that the Portuguese made for themselves in Malaysia because of their behavior. Portuguese sailors and spice traders engaged in brawls and drunkenness—habits that disgusted the locals:

> The uncouth, unruly and uncultured Portuguese of the time could not have impressed the Southeast Asians as being the torchbearers of European civilization. Even a great missionary, St. Francis Xavier, was so disgusted with their debaucherous way of life that he shook the dust of [Malaysia] from his feet vowing never to return to the cesspool of vices again.[27]

Roman Catholic missionaries of the Jesuit order who arrived in Vietnam in the eighteenth century, some two hundred years after the Portuguese, enjoyed a better reputation and a good deal more success. But the large number of Christian conversions so worried the Vietnamese ruling class, which was Buddhist, that between 1712 and 1720 Christianity was outlawed.

Later, when France ruled the country, Vietnamese Catholics enjoyed a good many new freedoms. But the French left in 1954, and Vietnam was cut in half by the Geneva agreement, setting the stage for the Vietnam War. Fearing retribution by the new government, over half a million northern Vietnamese Catholics fled south. Montagnard tribespeople, many of them Catholic, stayed in their villages but were particularly hard hit by the changes. Montagnard churches were closed and restrictions levied, though tribespeople continued to hold Sunday mass in their homes.

Catholicism in the Philippines

The Spanish brought Roman Catholicism to the Philippines when they arrived and took control of the islands in the sixteenth century. Not surprisingly, Spanish clergy found their conversion efforts hampered by their government's decision to tax any native baptized as a Catholic. The Filipinos balked and often regarded the priests with outright derision. However, the priests failed to discern the reason for

Cham Muslims Are Persecuted for Their Faith

Cambodia's Cham, descendants of the great Champa empire that once dominated the southern half of Vietnam, are devout Muslims who have incorporated their centuries-old traditions into their worship of Allah. They are also sectarians, followers of a branch of Islam called Imam San, after its founding leader. Members of the Imam San sect call themselves Kaum Juma'at, or the Friday group, because they pray only once, on Fridays. Most Muslims believe they must pray several times a day.

The Cham were driven out of their territory in the fifteenth century by ethnic Vietnamese, who were living to the north of Champa at the time. Most Cham fled to Cambodia, where about two hundred thousand live today. The Cham are fishermen, farmers, and boatbuilders, and most are quite poor.

They brought with them traditions and religious symbols that date all the way back to the empire's heyday. The Cham use these symbols to celebrate Imam San's birthday each year, decorating trees (much like Westerners decorate Christmas trees) with Champa religious symbols made from sugar-bread: the moon and stars, the Champa temple and calendar, and the Naga, Champa's mythical water serpent.

Perhaps the lowest point for the Cham in modern times happened during the Khmer Rouge regime in the 1970s. Thousands of Cham were killed and countless others forced from their homes. They were also forced to violate their Muslim beliefs by raising pigs and eating pork. One Cham leader told a Cambodian newspaper that his wife had been forced to raise a pig by the Khmer Rouge. When the pig died, they killed her, he said.

So few male Cham survived the Khmer Rouge bloodbath that tribe members now trace their lineage through their women. Cham women have also taken over many of the duties that men used to perform. Today's Cham mostly live in poverty, in bamboo huts with few adornments or domestic utensils.

Portuguese explorers brought Christianity to Southeast Asia in the 1500s. Churches, like the one pictured, are found throughout the region.

mischievous and humble; forward and villainous . . . full of compassion, but cruel . . . in the matters of sacred doctrine that are repeatedly taught them, difficult and inconstant; they go to church [but] . . . observe their [own] rituals . . . they are disrespectful of their priests.[28]

But disrespected or not, the clergy came to wield considerable influence in the community—and the nation. The Vatican sent a powerful representative to Manila, the islands' capital, and the church founded the region's oldest college, the College of St. Thomas, in 1645. The Spanish army, with express encouragement from the church, beat back the Muslim influence from the southern part of Luzon, the main island. One observer of that era expressed an opinion that of all the many layers of power, the clergy remained the most influential of all. The reason for this, he implied, was proximity. "The Governor-General is in Manila [far away], the King is in Spain [farther still] and God is in heaven [farthest of all]; but the priest is everywhere."[29]

Today's Missionaries

Christian missionaries to Southeast Asia have learned the hard way that interaction with the local culture can be fatal. As late as

such unkind words. In his book *The Philippines,* Filipino academic Onofre D. Corpuz quotes the bemused analysis of an eighteenth-century friar:

The nature of [the Filipinos] is a maze of contradictions and opposites . . . they are at one and the same time the 1970s, reports from Indonesia indicated that a group of Christian missionaries had been killed and eaten by a tribe of head-hunters. Tribespeople, it was said, suspected the missionaries of plotting to steal their land and take liberties with their women.

Many missionaries working today still find it difficult to find converts in the local population. A Dutch missionary, Gerritt Van Enk, reported in 1991 that after ten years of ministering to a Korowai tribe that lives near the Becking River in Indonesia, he had failed to baptize a single person. However, many successful missions still exist, even among the most remote of forest tribes. One particular success story belongs to the Crosiers, a Roman Catholic order from St. Paul, Minnesota. They have lived and worked among the Asmat of Irian Jaya, Indonesia, since 1958. They have adopted Asmat dress and customs, holding masses in tribal longhouses. The priests wear Asmat tooth necklaces and fur headbands in lieu of traditional priestly vestments. The Crosiers not only won the Asmat's devotion, but were able to repay the people's hospitality in an unexpected way.

During the 1960s, the Indonesian government was ready to outlaw Asmat feasts, carvings, and longhouses. The Crosiers acted as a go-between for the tribes and the government. Eventually, they persuaded the latter to lift their ban. Today, the Crosiers maintain a tribal museum at a settlement called Asmat. Some of their priests have lived with the Asmat for decades. The Asmat faithful still attend mass longhouse-style, the altar is made of a huge, oval tree trunk, and the figure of Jesus on the cross wears a crown of feathers, not thorns.

The Colonial Era Begins

Southeast Asia participated in cultural and religious exchanges with China and India for many years. Save for China's expansion into Vietnam during various points of its history, neither of these ancient countries had much interest in colonization. Thus, most of Southeast Asia's conflicts and problems remained internal for hundreds of years. The arrival of the Europeans, however, changed all that. The Westerners were bent on trade and on exploiting the Old World's vast and valuable resources. They were also bent on changing the lives and religions of its people, a process that is still going on today.

Chapter 5

A Road of Blood and Spices

Europeans made their first contacts with Southeast Asia in 1511. However, few Europeans came to the region for the next three hundred years. When they finally did start arriving, their purpose was twofold: to convert the local population to Christianity, and to make money by exploiting Southeast Asia's bounty of natural resources.

The long and complicated history of European colonialism in Southeast Asia may best be studied on a country-by-country basis by considering what motivated Western explorers and what impact Westerners had on the indigenous populations. The great changes the Europeans made in the region's landscape are important as well. For centuries, local tribespeople had worked with the land, adapting themselves to its challenges. Westerners, however, wanted to change the landscape to suit their needs. And they did change it forever, bringing railroads, modern weapons, and road systems, to name just a few examples.

First Contacts: The Portuguese

The spices that grew naturally on the islands of Indonesia were what first drew Portuguese sailors to that region in the early sixteenth century, when the Indonesian island chain was known as the Spice Islands. In those days it was believed, mistakenly, that spices could only be grown there and nowhere else on the earth.

These spices—pepper, nutmeg, and cloves—were highly prized in Europe for use in food preparation and preservation, and in making medicines. During the Middle Ages, spices flavored what would otherwise have been a very bland diet, for in those days there was no refrigeration and even the wealthy lived on pickled and salted fish and meat. Thus there was money to be made by importing spices, and the chance to do this drew the Portuguese to Indonesia in the sixteenth century.

"Portuguese explorations and conquest were inspired by the three Gs: gospel,

A painting depicts sixteenth-century Portuguese sailors exploring the coast of Indonesia.

gold and glory for their king,"[30] writes one historian. But the nation's push eastward put it in conflict with the Arab traders already doing business in the region. The Portuguese soon made sworn enemies of these business rivals, but not over money or territory. The Arabs were Muslim and therefore, in the eyes of the Catholic Por-

tuguese, infidels. The conflict between Arab Muslims and Portuguese Christians would last for decades.

However, Portugal did acquire an eastern trade route, holding it for more than one hundred years. The Portuguese kept their outposts mostly on the island nations, Malaysia and Indonesia, since mainland

A group of Banda dancers carry remnants of armor left by the Portuguese.

kingdoms were powerful enough then to drive away any challengers. Many individuals grew wealthy through the spice trade, but the Portuguese colonial empire was not to endure in the region. A complex set of cultural, political, and geographical factors contributed to a decline in the tiny Iberian nation's power, and by the end of the seventeenth century, Portugal had lost almost all of its properties in Southeast Asia.

The Dutch

The Dutch entered the spice trade in the mid-1600s and fared somewhat better than their predecessors. Unlike the Portuguese, they had no interest in converting the local peoples to Christianity. Their main interest was commerce, and as they took Indonesia away from Portugal, they were careful to pick the winning side in an ongoing battle between rival monarchies in Java. By the end of the seventeenth century, the monarchy that they favored had come to power in that province.

By working behind the scenes in the political system, the Dutch largely avoided any bloody conflicts between themselves and the islanders. Yet there was one horrendous exception to this pattern. Dutch traders considered the Bandanese people, a native tribe of spice traders who did business on the Asian mainland, to be rivals and wanted to get rid of them. After a long period of antagonistic action by the Dutch, the Bandanese felt obligated to fight back, with weapons. The Europeans then descended upon them and nearly eliminated the tribe. Bandanese were shot, hanged, or decapitated. Out of fifteen thousand tribal members, fewer than six hundred survived this slaughter. The Dutch now had the Indonesian spice trade to themselves.

Later, the Dutch also instituted a nonviolent change that would nonetheless have a major impact on the lives of native peoples. They introduced coffee and sugar, which are grown on plantations, to the islands. Soon many native peoples were working on these plantations, rather than

The Death of Magellan

Explorer Ferdinand Magellan faced starvation, turbulent seas, and a near mutiny. He overcame all these obstacles; however, he could *not* overcome a group of island warriors determined to kill him.

Magellan's journey around the world had begun two years before his death, in 1519. He left Spain determined to find a better route to the Spice Islands, now known as Indonesia. The route he took proved impractical—by way of Argentina and a strait that would one day bear his name—yet he would be the first European ever to set sail in the Pacific Ocean. In April 1521, he reached the Philippines and began a series of interactions with the natives. One tribal chief whom he befriended converted to Christianity. On April 26, Magellan's new friend sent him a message: He had been threatened by an overlord who would not recognize the king of Spain. He asked Magellan if he would send a boat and some of his men to help fight this enemy.

Magellan arrived personally with three boats and sixty men. When the overlord again refused to recognize Spain's sovereignty, Magellan and his men attacked. They burned homes in the local village to frighten the warriors, but the fire had the opposite effect. The tribespeople became so enraged that they shot a poisoned arrow into Magellan's leg. He was finally overwhelmed by the group of heavily armed natives.

The leader of the warrior party that killed Magellan, Lapulapu, became a hero. Today on Mactan, the island where the final battle took place, a large bronze statue of Lapulapu stands; he is considered the first Filipino to stand up to Western aggression. As for Magellan's crew, they pressed on without him, reaching their goal, the Spice Islands, in November 1521. They then headed home to Spain, becoming the first sailors ever to circle the world.

growing their own crops. One hundred years after the Dutch arrived, coffee and sugar exports were just as important as spices.

Spanish Conquerors

Of all the colonial powers who arrived in Southeast Asia before the nineteenth century, Spain undoubtedly had the biggest influence, even though they confined their presence to the Philippines. Ferdinand Magellan had claimed the Philippines for King Philip of Spain when he reached the islands during his round-the-world voyage in 1521. The Spaniards who followed him came to stay; they named the islands "Philippines" in honor of their king. They would rule from 1571 to 1898, when the Americans took over. The Philippines became the most Christian, as well as the most westernized, nation in Southeast Asia thanks to the Spaniards' influence.

Filipino islanders had largely been left alone for centuries. The storm-infested seas that surrounded their island homes had discouraged many visitors. Moreover, the spices that so attracted merchants to the region were not grown in the Philippines. In any event, few Filipino historical records are left from the early days, making it difficult to reconstruct the islands' past.

The Spaniards, however, left plenty of records behind. Their primary reason for controlling the Philippines was, at least at first, the galleon trade. Galleons are sailing ships, and the Spanish docked theirs in the natural harbor located at what is now the capital city of the Philippines, Manila. While docked at Manila, the galleons would be loaded up with Chinese porcelain, silks, spices, ivory, and jade, all purchased from regional traders. The ships were then sailed to Acapulco, Mexico, another Spanish property. The goods were then sent on to buyers in North America and Europe, and the ships loaded up again, this time with silver and bullion used to pay for the goods just delivered. The Spanish galleons then headed back to the islands so that the cycle could start up again.

Spaniards who arrived prior to the eighteenth century purchased large tracts of lands, known as *encomiendas*, or royal estates; those who arrived later were encouraged by the king to live in cities. And as time went on, the Spanish became more interested in exploiting their colony's natural resources. They cut timber from the lowland forests, planted sugar cane on large chunks of land, and mined gold from the hills. All of these efforts brought them into conflict with a local people known as the Igorots—an umbrella name for a group of tribes, including the Bontoc and Kalinga, that lives in the Cordillera region of the main Filipino island. Some tribespeople agreed to work with the Spanish, while others fiercely resisted. The Igorot paid dearly for this resistance: The Spanish burned their homes and crops and tried to drive them out of their homelands. But in 350 years of Spanish rule, this effort never quite succeeded, and the Igorot fiercely clung to their homes.

The surrender of Rangoon to British troops in 1824.

The British in Malaysia and Burma

Britain gained a foothold in Southeast Asia in unlikely fashion: as an unintended consequence of the Napoleonic Wars. The Dutch king, William V, who had fled to England when Napoleon's army occupied the Netherlands, allowed his hosts to take over all Dutch properties in Southeast Asia. The British arrived there in 1811, but thirteen years later signed a treaty with Holland that gave back some of the territories. The British took care to keep Singapore and parts of Malaysia and Indonesia for themselves. The Dutch controlled much of the island of Borneo, but in 1841 an Englishman named James Brooke staked a claim for himself on the northern half of the island, in what would become the state of Sarawak. He named himself rajah, or king, and he and his family became known as the white rajahs of Sarawak. The Brookes ruled their personal kingdom until after World War II, when Brooke's grandnephew signed it over to the British empire.

James Brooke was able to grab the land for himself because of the inner turmoil in the region and because the Dutch unaccountably failed to drive him away.

Throughout their years on Borneo, Brooke and his family appeared to gain a real affection for the island and its people; eventually, they even considered themselves Malaysians. Margaret Brooke, the wife of James's nephew Charles, who succeeded him as rajah in 1868, describes her feelings for the Malaysian people in her autobiography: "Little by little I lost some of my European ideas and became more of a mixture between a Dyak and a Malay. The extraordinary idea which English people entertain as to an insuperable bar existing between the white and coloured races, even in those days of my youth, appeared to me to be absurd and nonsensical."[31]

But the family's affinity for their adopted home did not prevent them from quashing uprisings when they arose. The Iban and Kenyah were local tribespeople who occasionally chafed at Brooke's reign, particularly when he tried to force them to give up headhunting. Brooke also employed ethnic Chinese to work in his mining operations; the presence of foreigners on Iban land infuriated the Borneo natives; conflict between the miners and Iban warriors was a problem Brooke often had to deal with.

The British empire took a hands-off attitude toward Brooke and his personal kingdom. They had a full plate elsewhere in the region and were loath to expand their influence further, at least until the 1860s. Political and social unrest in central Asia, home to their prime property, India, changed their point of view. The independent kingdom of Burma bordered India and therefore, in the minds of the British, became a logical buffer against the French, who were expanding their influence in Vietnam and seeking out commercial markets in China. In addition, the British were eager to incorporate Burma into their global empire. With these factors in mind, Britain engaged Burma in a series of wars that lasted until 1885, when the Burmese monarchy was abolished. Like India, Burma was now a colony under British control.

The French

In the mid–nineteenth century, the French decided to go to Vietnam and Cambodia in part for religious reasons. Harsh anti-Catholic sentiment was still widespread in the region, and to the French desire for a share in Southeast Asia's riches was added the desire to help fellow Roman Catholics. French armies conquered the lower half of Vietnam in 1862 and renamed it Cochin China. They subsequently extended their rule over the central part of the country, which they renamed Annam. Twenty-one years after conquering Cochin China, the French marched into northern Vietnam and took Hanoi. The northern region became Tonkin and the name "Vietnam" disappeared from official use. Cochin China, Annam, and Tonkin were eventually combined with Laos and Cambodia (which had come under French rule during the same time) in a region that became known as French Indochina.

Vietnam had long been used to outsiders: China had been its master during ancient times, and then again for a generation in the fifteenth century. But the Chinese rarely interfered with daily life. France, on the other hand, wanted to turn its new colonial subjects into French gentlemen—Catholic French gentlemen. Vietnam's hill people, the Montagnards, showed no signs of wanting to become gentlemen or French, but they had at least converted to Catholicism in large numbers. For this reason they enjoyed a fairly good relationship with the French. To the south, in the Spanish-ruled Philippines, however, relations between colonizers and their subjects were far from good.

America in the Philippines

By the late 1890s, Filipinos had had enough of Spanish domination. In 1897 their leaders led an uprising against Spain and proclaimed the islands a republic. The United States, itself at war with Spain, promised arms and support to the rebels. American forces, led by Admiral George Dewey, landed in the Philippines in 1899. Once they landed, however, the Americans negotiated a secret treaty with Spain that transferred ownership of the Philippines to the United States.

A fierce battle would erupt between America and the rebels. American forces killed or impoverished any civilian populations suspected of supporting the uprising. On the Filipino island of Marinduque an entire population would be rounded up into concentration camps, their villages and crops burned by U.S. troops. At another point in the conflict, an American general by the name of Jacob F. Smith gave this command to his troops. "Kill and burn," he said. "Kill and burn, and the more you burn, the more you please me. This is no time to take prisoners. Kill [all children] over ten."[32]

A painting portrays America's 1899 involvement in the Philippines as unleashing vicious dogs on native rebels.

The war between America and the guerrillas officially ended in 1902. Skirmishes between local tribespeople and the new government continually flared up, with about three hundred thousand Filipinos being held in concentration camps. When hostilities finally ceased, six hundred thousand Filipinos, about one-seventh of the entire population, had been killed.

America had never been a colonial power before, and her reasons for taking over the Philippines were complicated. Many national leaders at that time still believed in a concept called manifest destiny: The United States was meant to push westward, as it had across the North American continent, and stake out its influence elsewhere in the globe. Many believed that this scenario was in accordance with God's will.

On the economic front, America also hoped to make the Philippines a stopping point on the trade route it was developing in the Far East.

World War II and Independence

America, Great Britain, and France, which were major players in Southeast Asia at the beginning of the twentieth century, were also greatly affected by events in the Pacific during World War II. In December 1941, the Japanese attacked Pearl Harbor, Hawaii, and a few days later invaded the Philippines. After a few months of fighting, General Douglas MacArthur, the American chief military adviser, was forced to flee to Australia. Although posing as the liberators of the Philippines, the Japanese were in reality an occupying force, and the people rose up against them. For the next two years Filipinos conducted guerrilla warfare against Japan and waited for U.S. troops to return.

Japan, having succeeded in the Philippines, moved quickly into Indochina. The French did little at first when the Japanese occupied their colonies. But in 1944, a group of French commandos parachuted into Laos, determined to liberate French Indochinese territory from the Japanese. Once there they found an ally on the ground: the Laotian Hmong.

The Hmong had gotten on fairly well with the French, siding with them against their traditional enemy, the Lao, a lowland people who lived in what is today the country of Laos. Taking an instant dislike to their Japanese conquerors, who treated them cruelly, the Hmong offered themselves up as guides and messengers for the French commandos. They volunteered to be trained as guerrilla warriors, and when the French were in danger, hid and protected them, usually at great risk to themselves.

One of these commandos, Second Lieutenant Maurice Gauthier, came away with vivid memories of the Hmong:

> The Hmong could walk eight to ten miles an hour for 48 hours. I considered myself in top physical shape, but in the early days I had great difficulty in keeping the Hmong pace. . . . I was amazed that the Hmong approached a mountaintop by heading straight to its

peak. . . . One day, I asked the men with me why they always walked straight to the top of the mountain. . . . One man answered simply, "That's where we're going."[33]

Meanwhile, Japanese troops were spreading their influence elsewhere in the region. They landed in Indonesia in 1942, and two years later, drove the British out of Burma. Japan always poised itself as a liberator during these invasions, but once in place, they assumed the reins of power instead of granting freedom to the residents, just as Western nations before them had done. They incurred particular hatred in Burma by desecrating pagodas and burning scriptures of the Burmese Buddhists. Burma's rebels eventually contacted their old masters, the British, and put together their own conglomerate. The Anti-Fascist People's Freedom League, or

The Slow Destruction of Laos's Hmong

The U.S. involvement in Laos officially ended in 1973, but the travails of the Hmong of Laos had just begun. The United States had abandoned this loyal ally when it pulled troops from Vietnam and elsewhere in Southeast Asia, and the Pathet Lao were now in charge in Laos. The Communists vowed to wipe out their old enemy, the Hmong, who were fleeing Laos by the thousands. Their departure was well advised, for Laotian Communists and their Vietnamese allies massacred many Hmong tribespeople and rounded up others to be tortured and imprisoned in forced labor and "reeducation" camps. Hmong women captured by the Vietnamese were repeatedly raped and humiliated in front of the male prisoners. Those Hmong who survived came away with heartrending stories: One young girl who made it safely to the United States told of how the Communists had ex-

ecuted thirty-three members of her family. She had been seriously wounded and was able to escape only because the Pathet Lao had left her for dead.

Tens of thousands of Hmong eventually settled in the United States. Most went to large, industrial cities and most experienced severe cultural shock. Because so many Hmong men had been killed in the war, the men who were left took second and third wives; but in the United States they are only allowed to be married to one wife at a time. Thus, many families were forced to break up to live in safety in America.

Today's Hmong are still fighting a battle—to preserve their cultural traditions in a changing and hostile world. Large Hmong communities have since grown up in Minneapolis and St. Paul, Minnesota, and in other U.S. cities.

AFPFL, which included a group of Burmese Communists, rose up against Japan, with help from Britain, in 1945. The Japanese withdrew in May of that year, and the AFPFL controlled most of Burma. The British insisted on installing an interim government of their own, but it was already too late; the old colonial system had been destroyed forever. The British finally left for good in 1948, and Burma was an independent nation again.

General MacArthur and his troops liberated the Philippines in 1944, a victory that was greatly aided by the guerrillas' resistance campaign that had been in place since 1942. In 1946, two years after their day of liberation, full independence was granted to the Filipinos. They were the first colonial territory to win independence from their masters.

A Vietnamese Drive for Independence

Whereas the British and Americans withdrew from their colonies in Southeast Asia, the French stayed. And like the peoples of Burma and the Philippines, the Vietnamese wanted independence. Within the country's new nationalist movement were a number of homegrown Communists, including a man named Ho Chi Minh.

Ho Chi Minh had spent part of his youth in England and Paris, where he was active in the French Socialist Party. In 1930 he helped to form the Indochina Communist Party (ICP), but after a failed uprising he was arrested and sent to prison. During World War II, however, Chinese Nationalist leader Chiang Kai-shek managed to get Ho released from prison. In addition to providing charismatic leadership to the local resistance effort as Chiang had intended, Ho founded a new political movement, the Vietminh, aimed at freeing his country of all outside rulers. After Japan surrendered to the Allies in 1945, Vietnam proclaimed itself a republic. Ho's Vietminh comrades elected him to head the new nation's provisional government; but independence was short-lived. Chinese troops entered the north end of the country, and the British went to the south. When the French tried to reassert their colonial rights, Ho Chi Minh reluctantly welcomed them back, so eager was he to rid the country of the Chinese.

The new agreement stipulated that France would recognize Vietnam as a free state through part of a political entity known as the Indochinese Federation. France had no real desire to give up its sovereignty over Vietnam, however, and failed to honor important parts of the agreement. Thus it was not long before war broke out, with the Vietminh receiving help from their fellow Communist Nationalists, the Pathet Lao in neighboring Laos.

The French withdrew in 1954, but only after the signing of an agreement turning over North Vietnam to the Vietminh. In South Vietnam the French installed Ngo Dinh Diem, a man who enjoyed U.S. support, to run the country. Ngo, who was pro-French and pro-Catholic, making him

Ho Chi Minh, hero of the Vietnamese Communist movement, prepares for a mission against the French as a young guerrilla.

popular with the Montagnards, cracked down hard on Communist dissenters. He also forbade Buddhist holidays and festivities, a move that eventually led to his downfall. Vietnam's Buddhists organized themselves into the General Buddhist As-sociation to protest Ngo's anti-Buddhist policies. Ngo's intransigence toward Vietnam's Buddhists, who were in the majority in that country, eventually cost him U.S. and French support. Neither country interfered when Ngo and his brother,

Nhu, were assassinated by Vietnamese generals who wanted to overthrow the government.

Tensions between North and South Vietnam increased, and in 1964, America became involved, following reports that a North Vietnamese ship had attacked an American ship, the *Maddox*, in the Gulf of Tonkin. The United States retaliated with a lengthy bombing campaign. By 1967 U.S. troops in Vietnam numbered half a million. The bloodiest battle of the war, the 1968 Tet Offensive, resulted in heavy losses on both sides.

Fighting spread to otherwise neutral Cambodia after a military coup sent the prince into exile, and American and South Vietnamese troops entered that country in 1970. After an exhaustive fight, the American government decided to withdraw, particularly since the war had become so unpopular with much of the American public. In 1975, South Vietnam was overrun and conquered by Communist forces from the north.

Indigenous Tribes Are Devastated

The Vietnam conflict was long, bloody, and tragic for everyone involved. But its effect on the indigenous tribes of Vietnam, Cambodia, and Laos was nothing

The Vietnam War displaced millions of indigenous people, like this family fleeing to safety.

short of disastrous. The effects of the war still linger today in Vietnam. Roy C. Russell, a former American military officer who visited Montagnard territory in 2001, reported that villages were protesting the land and religious rights they lost in the wake of that conflict. Some Montagnards are still prosperous, he said, but much of their traditional culture had vanished:

> Magazines provided by Air Vietnam for its passengers feature colorful pictures and romantic accounts of Montagnard ceremonies, complete with traditional dress, music and dance. If such things exist it must be only in a [specially created] village held in reserve to entertain the tourists. We certainly did not see anything that came even remotely close to these colorful magazine accounts.[34]

The Vietnam conflict left a particularly bloody imprint in Cambodia. After the U.S. withdrawal, Cambodian leader Pol Pot and his Khmer Rouge led a three-year reign of terror. Millions of Cambodians died, including among them the descendants of the great Champa empire, one of the earliest Southeast Asian kingdoms. The Cham, who are Muslims, were a targeted group during Pol Pot's purge. It is estimated that one hundred thousand of them lost their lives.

The stories of Pol Pot's reign are still being told by survivors of the era when thousands of Cambodians who were transported to rural areas, where they spent fifteen to eighteen hours a day farming rice or building canals and dikes. They each received only seven hundred grams of rice a day, and many died of overwork or starvation. "We ate grass; there were even people who ate [dead bodies]; they tried to dig down [in the graves] and just get a bit of flesh,"[35] a survivor says in an interview published years later.

An Era Ends

The colonial era is over, the horrors of the Cold War have ebbed, and yet many indigenous tribes still struggle to find a place in the modern world. The majority of tribespeople have had to adopt Western ways in some form or another—sometimes housing, sometimes a job that pays regular wages. Yet even with the compromises these men and women make, their position in society is precarious at best.

Chapter 6

Pain and Progress

Every year, the modern world encroaches on the lives of indigenous tribespeople more and more. Tourism alone brings thousands of new people into Southeast Asia annually. Then there are the mining, logging, and oil companies, which seek to harvest the region's natural resources, many of which are located on tribal land. National governments, particularly those in Indonesia and Myanmar, have disrupted the lives of native peoples through resettlement or political upheaval.

Even tribespeople able to live a fairly peaceful lifestyle are under constant pressure to conform to Western ways. They work in low-paying jobs that keep them in poverty, and their children often explore Western culture with open-minded enthusiasm.

"The long-term effects of modern development projects on indigenous peoples are all too often catastrophic," author Julian Burger writes in his book *The Gaia Atlas of First Peoples*. "Once divorced from their lands, their independent way of life, and group support, they seek survival within the dominant, national society. Yet when they do, it is usually at the lowest level. . . . Indigenous peoples are offered the least schooling, medical care and welfare, the worst housing and lowest salaries."[36]

However, there are signs of hope, particularly in the numbers of indigenous organizations and even resistance movements. Indigenous peoples, like peoples everywhere, are learning that there is safety and progress in numbers.

Resettlement and Violence in Myanmar

Indigenous tribes are so strongly tied to their homelands that losing them is traumatic to the very fabric of their identities. In Myanmar, political unrest has uprooted tribes, like the Karen, Kachin, and Shan, from the territory where they have lived for generations. Burma, now called Myanmar, has been under the control of a military government since 1988. That government has forced its citizens, including hill tribespeople, into forced labor situations. Tribes like the Karen, who have been fighting for years for an independent state, are considered a threat to the government and have been forced off their land. At least five hundred thousand Burmese have fled the country since 1988. Most Karen refugees have fled over the border to Thailand. A refugee who at age sixty-eight made it to a Thai refugee camp relates this story of horror to a researcher. "There were about 300 people including women and children in our group. One of our friends stepped on a land mine, his leg was blown off and he died. The [Myanmar] army chased us, we walked day and night in the jungle."[37]

Humanitarian aid groups have recorded many instances where Karen, Shan, and Kachin have been tortured, raped, or killed. Karen resistance has spilled violently into Thailand. In January 2000, a group of Karen seized a hospital in the Thai town of Ratchaburi, holding more than two hundred patients and staff hostage. They demanded that Thailand provide medical care to other members of their group and an open border to other refugees. All the Karen gunmen were killed when Thai soldiers stormed the hospital.

A group of indigenous dancers performs at a rally in Jakarta supporting tribal independence.

Refugees from the Karen tribe in Burma flee across the Thai–Burmese border.

Resettlement and Oppression in Indonesia

Indonesia's current problems stem from the aftermath of World War II. Indonesia had become an independent nation, and its government at the time sought to combine its far-flung islands and peoples into a cohesive society. To do that, they would have to gain control of some ethnically diverse peoples. Government officials occupied what was then known as West Papua, historically a Dutch possession, and renamed it Irian Jaya. They forbid West Papuans from identifying themselves as such, and elsewhere in the country, racial distinctions were abolished. All native residents of the archipelago, consisting of more than three thousand islands, are Indonesians now.

Indonesia has long been rich in timber and metal deposits—something that the government has continually tried to exploit. But another strategy has proved equally disruptive to the lives of native peoples: that of resettlement. Historically around 60 percent of Indonesia's 170 million-plus people have lived on only 7 percent of the available land. The government came up with a plan to move millions of villagers from the densely populated central islands of Java, Madura, and Bali to the sparsely populated outer islands of

Borneo (Indonesia controls a southern province known as Kalimantan), Sulawesi, and Sumatra. The relocation of strangers into their homeland has brought a good deal of turmoil into the lives of people like the Dani and Dyak, and has in many cases

led to some bloody conflicts between the newcomers and the indigenous populations.

Modern-Day Mining
From gold mines in the Philippines to tin mines in Malaysia, Southeast Asia's

A Burmese Independence Movement

The withdrawal of British troops from Burma, now known as Myanmar, led to the birth of the Karen independence movement. The Karen, along with other hill tribes, such as the Kachin and Shan, were living as minorities in their own country, in the mountainous and remote region that borders Thailand. For the most part they had maintained good relations with their British rulers. But they feared that rule by their own countrymen would marginalize them in Burmese society and cause them to lose their traditional ways of life.

The Karen's first try at independence occurred in 1948, with the support of their old friends, the British. Highly victorious at first, the Karen came close to overthrowing the government. However, the Burmese army eventually beat them back. The Karen and the Burmese government fought sporadically throughout the 1960s. The Karen were eventually joined by other tribal independence movements begun by the Shan, the Kachin, and others. All of these groups, including the Karen, wanted an independent homeland and self-government. In 1975 they formed a coalition called the National

Democratic Front (NDF). At first the coalition and the Burmese government tried to negotiate a peace agreement; but settlement talks soon failed. By the early 1980s, Burma and the NDF were fighting openly. In March 1984 a particularly vicious attack by government forces against the Karen sent thousands of refugees spilling over the border into Thailand. Karen National Liberation Army headquarters were destroyed during that fight.

The Karen struck back four years later by seizing territory around the city of Rangoon. Burmese soldiers arrived to win it back, though they still had to cope with the land mines buried by retreating tribespeople. In 1989, following a military coup born of the preceding year's violence, the name of the country was changed to Myanmar.

The struggle of the Karen goes on today, though unlike other groups, they have avoided funding their movement via the opium trade. Instead the Karen earn money by taxing the black market goods that are smuggled across the border through the mountains that encompass the area where they have traditionally lived.

treasure trove of natural resources has long attracted Western entrepreneurs. Mining continues today in the region, bringing with it a host of environmental problems. There are other issues as well, as illustrated by the experience of an American mining company, Freeport-McMoran, which mined gold and copper in the western half of Indonesia's Irian Jaya province. The mines were on the land of the local indigenous peoples, the Dani, Moni, Amungme, and Komoro. The work was done with little consideration for them or their way of life, and all the high-paying jobs in the company went to outsiders. Tensions between the two sides boiled over in the late 1990s when a mining vehicle accidentally struck a local tribal member. A riot ensued, with hundreds of tribespeople using traditional weapons—sticks, spears, and knives—to ransack buildings and break windows. They shut down the mine and local airport for three days. A tribal spokesman sent this angry message to the company's owners: "You and your workers live in luxury on our property. We, who own the rights to the property, sleep on rubbish. Therefore, from today, we don't give you permission for this company and close it."[38]

The mines eventually reopened, after which Freeport-McMoran agreed to open a job-training center for the local people.

Logging in the Spice Islands

Spices were the original lure for the adventurers who first explored the islands of Southeast Asia. But in today's world, timber is one of the biggest draws. The rain forests, which proved so nourishing for so long to tribes like the Penan, the Kayan, and the Moi, are now a place for timber companies to make money. Wood and forest products from the islands are sent all over the world, with Japan being a particularly large market.

Malaysia contains the world's oldest forests, with some dating back 150 million years; yet over a third of Sarawak forest was wiped out over a thirty-year period. In Indonesia, logging in the Irian Jaya province is taking place on tribal lands and making it more difficult for tribespeople to practice their traditional ways of life. "All the streams have dried up or become muddy," a Moi tribesman told a journalist who had come to investigate the effects of logging. "The fish we used to catch have disappeared. Tearing down our forest is like tearing out our hearts."[39]

Widespread logging has a serious impact on the environment, bringing about soil erosion and other problems. However, some indigenous tribespeople have decided to turn the demand for lumber to their advantage. Asmat tribespeople have been known to cut down trees themselves and sell them for three thousand Indonesian rupiahs, or $1.30 U.S., per tree stump. They use the money to buy radios and clothes, and to send their children to school; exposure to Western culture has given them a taste for these things. Other Asmat lament this practice, however.

Endangered Species, Endangered People

As Southeast Asia's wilderness areas continue to shrink, it becomes apparent that the indigenous human inhabitants are not the only ones whose futures are being threatened. Animal species that have coexisted with native tribes for centuries are also disappearing at an alarming rate.

The Indochinese tiger is one of these species. This magnificent big cat has historically been found in hilly and mountainous terrain, mostly in Thailand but also in Burma, southern China, Laos, Vietnam, and peninsular Malaysia. The Indochinese tiger has always been a reclusive animal. Nonetheless, scientists believe less than two thousand of them still survive in the wild, mostly because of hunting and the shrinking of their habitat.

Widespread logging on the island of Borneo has also threatened the habitat of Southeast Asia's only great ape, the orangutan. Orangutans, which live in northern Sumatra, died in great numbers when forest fires swept through the jungles of Malaysia and Indonesia in 1997 and 1998. They are also under constant threat by poachers.

Some of the most remarkable bird species in the world live in Southeast Asia, and these, too, are beginning to disappear. The beautifully colored bird of paradise, called bird of the sun by Malaysians, is slaughtered for its skin and its feathers; at least fifty thousand of them disappear from the region each year. Since only males are taken—they are the sex with the more colorful feathers—breeding rates have gone down drastically. Live birds of paradise are also captured and sold in the West, where they fetch as much as thirty thousand dollars apiece.

Some indigenous tribes in the region are contributing to the problem by trapping or killing these animals themselves. The reason for this destruction is simple: The black market for animal parts or feathers—some of which are believed to have healing properties—is quite lucrative. And as farmland and hunting grounds are lost to development, tribespeople are left with few other ways to earn a living.

Orangutans interact with humans at a research preserve in Sumatra.

79

Tribespeople pose with a Western tourist, an indication of the infusion of Western culture into indigenous societies.

"Our people need things from the outside. I can't pretend not," says one tribesman. "But can't we find a way to provide them without cutting down our trees?"[40]

Tribal Education

Western culture has permeated even the remote parts of Indonesia inhabited by the Asmat people. The young, particularly, are fascinated with Western ideas and entertainment. Travelers tell of television sets in jungle homes, and tribal elders bemoan the fact that young people are more likely to learn Western sports than they are tribal traditions.

But indigenous groups elsewhere in Southeast Asia are seeking to change that. Tuenjai Deetes, a spokesperson for the hill tribes of Thailand, explained in a 2000 interview how the newly created Hill Area Development Foundation (HADF) would help establish locally run schools for tribal children: "The general aim is to offer access to the formal education system. However, we also try to instill the children with a deep sense of pride in their history and culture, so that they won't blindly assimilate the ways of the mainstream society."[41] One of the ways the foundation plans to do this is to integrate tribal knowledge into the regular Thai curriculum.

Tourism: The Good and the Bad

Southeast Asia, with its incredible physical beauty and rich cultural heritage, is becoming a mecca for tourists. Tourists spend money in the region and come away with a new appreciation for different cultures. Tourism has its downside, though, particularly in the low-paying jobs it generates—jobs that are often filled by unskilled local tribespeople seeking to enter the job market.

Activists like Deetes charge that it is the touring companies that earn the real dollars, while indigenous peoples, who have

An Igorot Hero

It was the spring of 1980 when the Igorot people of the Philippines decided to fight back. The government of Ferdinand Marcos was finalizing plans to build a series of hydroelectric dams on the Chico River. These dams would provide electric power via the water current, but the flooding process associated with them would submerge entire villages and leave eighty-five thousand Igorot homeless.

Tribal elder Macliing Dulag, a father of six, pleaded with government authorities not to build the dams, stating that ownership of the land had come down to the Igorot through their ancestors. The government officials refused to listen, but Dulag, undaunted, began walking up and down the Chico River, urging villagers to resist. He was having some success organizing opposition to the project. But on April 24, 1980, a group of government soldiers who had heard of his activities came to arrest him. They knocked on the door in the middle of the night. While Dulag was climbing out of his bed and putting on his clothes, the soldiers fired through the door, killing him instantly. The soldier who shot Dulag was arrested, tried, and convicted, but after the trial the government quietly transferred him to another region, where he went on with his career.

Dulag's death galvanized his people. After the Igorot organized, protested, and vandalized dam-building equipment, violence erupted. A Roman Catholic bishop who lived in the region wrote to the Marcos government, pleading for the tribespeople to be left alone. Construction crews finally walked off the job, fearing for their own safety. The Cordillera Peoples Alliance (named for the Cordillera region, where the Igorot live) continued their activism, convinced that the government would return with other plans if they let down their guard.

The Igorot continue to meet annually on April 24, Cordillera Day, to remember their hero and martyr, Dulag.

A peasant with oxcarts crosses the Moei River from Thailand to Burma. Preserving traditional ways is a struggle for the indigenous people of Southeast Asia.

increasingly become tourist attractions themselves, come away with little. Others say, however, that tourism may be the region's best hope for preserving lands and lifestyles. Tourism dollars have convinced governments to preserve parkland, some of which is home to indigenous tribespeople. An example of this is the Wasur National Park in Indonesia. It covers 1 million acres of savannah, lowland forests, swamp, and beach—almost the size of Everglades National Park. Some twenty-five hundred people live within its borders; most of them belong to the Kanuma and Marind tribes.

Remote tribes like the Asmat have also been used as a tourist destination on a limited basis. These former headhunters have become so accustomed to visitors that they will sell them their native crafts. David Fanning, a writer who accompanied rock star Mick Jagger on a visit to the Asmat, came away with mixed feelings about the encounter. He cannot avoid the realization that each encounter with Westerners brings changes to Asmat culture, and he suggests that his visit benefited him more than it did his hosts:

> I want to believe . . . that we've done no harm. But I can't help feeling that I've been the agent of change [in their lives]. I have had the extraordinary privilege of being one of the few Westerners to touch the lives of the villagers . . . but I worry about the next few [Westerners]. And the ones that will follow. What will we each take away? What will we leave?[42]

The Drive for Autonomy

An increasing number of indigenous tribes are banding together in wider organizations, hoping to direct their future in more effective ways. The Philippines is home to two indigenous organizations, the National Federation of Indigenous Peoples and Cordillera Peoples Alliance. Filipino activists overcame two major dam projects on the Chico and Abulog Rivers, forcing reconsideration and eventual withdrawal of World Bank and Japanese government funding of these projects. Other victories include the closing of a logging and pulp production project and blocking plans by other timber and mining companies.

The plight of indigenous peoples worldwide has also received attention from such international groups as the International Labour Organization (ILO), Amnesty International, and the UN High Commissioner for Refugees.

Outside organizations like the Anti-Slavery Society and Survival International in the United Kingdom have begun to help, publishing information on, and raising funds for, indigenous peoples around the world.

Hoping for a Foothold

Indigenous tribes of Southeast Asia are looking to claim a foothold for themselves in the modern world. They have known great struggles and have seen much of their way of life vanish over the past few centuries. But tribespeople continue to believe that diligence and a willingness to demand what is theirs will ensure them a brighter future.

Notes

Chapter 1: The Tribes of Southeast Asia

1. Peter Kunstadter, "Spirits of Change Capture the Karens," *National Geographic,* February 1972, p. 283.
2. Anne De Henning Singh, "Sea Gypsies of the Philippines," *National Geographic,* May 1976, p. 664.
3. Eric Hansen, "The Nomads of Gunung," *Natural History,* April 1998, p. 34.
4. Hansen, "The Nomads of Gunung," p. 34.
5. Hansen, "The Nomads of Gunung," p. 35.
6. George Steinmetz, "Irian Jaya's People of the Trees," *National Geographic,* February 1996, p. 43.

Chapter 2: The Family Circle

7. Howard Sochurek, "Vietnam's Montagnards," *National Geographic,* April 1968, p. 464.
8. Peter Kunstadter, "Spirits of Change Capture the Karens," p. 283.
9. Quoted in Stan Sesser, *The Lands of Charm and Cruelty: Travels in Southeast Asia.* New York: Alfred A. Knopf, 1993, p. 256.
10. De Henning Singh, "Sea Gypsies of the Philippines," p. 677.

11. Dean C. Worcester, "Non-Christian Peoples of the Philippine Islands," *National Geographic,* November 1913, p. 1,229.
12. Quoted in Margaret Brooke, *My Life in Sarawak.* London: Methuen, 1913.
13. Sesser, *The Lands of Charm and Cruelty,* p. 256.

Chapter 3: Lances and Longhouses

14. Dean C. Worcester, "Head-Hunters of Northern Luzon," *National Geographic,* September 1912, p. 977.
15. Quoted in Sochurek, "Vietnam's Montagnards," p. 464.
16. Quoted in "Montagnards of the Central Highlands of Vietnam." www.landscaper.net.
17. Sesser, *The Lands of Charm and Cruelty,* p. 89.
18. Quoted in Jane Hamilton-Merritt, *Tragic Mountains: The Hmong, the Americans, and the Secret Wars for Laos, 1942–1992.* Bloomington: Indiana University Press, 1993, p. 212.
19. Patrick Walters, "Headhunting Again in Borneo," *World Press Review,* May 1997, p. 39.
20. Quoted in William W. Bevis, *Borneo Log: The Struggle for Sarawak's Forests.* Seattle: University of Washington Press, 1995, p. 157.

21. Quoted in Sesser, *The Lands of Charm and Cruelty,* p. 245.

Chapter 4: Nature Has a Soul

22. De Henning Singh, "Sea Gypsies of the Philippines," p. 667.

23. "The Mentawai, Indonesia." www.caske2000.org.

24. Quoted in Kunstadter, "Spirits of Change Capture the Karens," p. 283.

25. Quoted in Kunstadter, "Spirits of Change Capture the Karens," p. 284.

26. Quoted in Sochurek, "Vietnam's Montagnards," p. 463.

27. D.R. Sardesai, *Southeast Asia, Past and Present.* Boulder, CO: Westview Press, 1989, p. 62.

28. Onofre D. Corpuz, *The Philippines.* Englewood Cliffs, NJ: Prentice-Hall, 1965, pp. 38–39.

29. Corpuz, *The Philippines,* p. 45.

Chapter 5: A Road of Blood and Spices

30. Sardesai, *Southeast Asia, Past and Present,* p. 61.

31. Quoted in Brooke, *My Life in Sarawak.*

32. Quoted in Sardesai, *Southeast Asia, Past and Present,* p. 149.

33. Quoted in Hamilton-Merritt, *Tragic Mountains,* p. 31.

34. "Montagnards Revisited: In Search of the Past." www.cudenver.edu.

35. Quoted in Marie Alexandrine Martin, *Cambodia: A Shattered Society,* trans. by Mark W. McLeod. Berkeley: University of California Press, 1994, p. 175.

Chapter 6: Pain and Progress

36. Julian Burger, *The Gaia Atlas of First Peoples: A Future for the Indigenous World.* London: Gaia Books, 1990, p. 82.

37. Quoted in Jana Mason, *No Way In, No Way Out: Internal Displacement in Burma.* Washington, DC: U.S. Committee for Refugees, 2000, p. 15.

38. Quoted in Art Davidson, *Endangered Peoples.* San Francisco: Sierra Club Books, 1993, p. 172.

39. Quoted in Steinmetz, "Irian Jaya's People of the Trees," p. 33.

40. Quoted in Eyal Press, "Jim Bob's Indonesian Misadventure: A U.S. Mining Company Clashes with Indigenous Peoples," *Progressive,* June 1996, p. 34.

41. Quoted in Ethirajan Anbarasan, "Tuenjai Deetes: A Bridge to the Hill Tribes," *The Unesco Courier,* October 2000, p. 49.

42. David Fanning, "Cannibals on Main Street [visiting Asmat people in Irian Jaya and cruising Indonesia]," *Condé Nast Traveler,* June 1996, pp. 105–106.

For Further Reading

Books

Edward Gargan, *The River's Tale: A Year on the Mekong.* New York: Alfred A. Knopf, 2002. Former *New York Times* journalist Gargan traveled three thousand miles down the Mekong River, through China, Tibet, Burma, Laos, Thailand, Cambodia, and Vietnam. Most of his daily experiences involved interactions with peoples who have lived on the riverbanks for generations. For mature readers.

Margaret Landon, *Anna and the King of Siam.* New York: HarperPerennial, 1943. The book that inspired two movies and the hit musical *The King and I* tells the true story of Englishwoman Anna Leonowens, who served as tutor to the Thai royal family. The book details in particular her relationships with Thai king Mongkut and crown prince Chulalongkorn.

Library of Nations, *Southeast Asia.* Amsterdam: Time-Life Books, 1987. Overview of the nations of Southeast Asia and their indigenous populations as well as historical and religious perspectives.

Charles Lindsay, *Mentawai Shaman: Keeper of the Rainforest: Man, Nature, and Spirits in Remote Indonesia.* New York: Aperture Books, 1993. Photo essay on the Mentawai people includes eighty photographs, a historical essay by anthropologist Reimar Schefold, and excerpts from the author's diaries. For mature readers.

John S. Major, *The Land and People of Malaysia and Brunei.* New York: HarperCollins Children's Books, 1991. Major's book gives an account of Malaysia's history from ancient to modern times with many engaging sidebars on various aspects of Malaysia's culture.

Evelyn Peplow, *The Philippines.* Kowloon, Hong Kong: Odyssey Publications, 1999. Although intended as a travel guide, Pep-low's book contains several essays by authors familiar with the islands and several short but informative historical narratives.

Shelton Woods, *Vietnam: An Illustrated History.* New York: Hippocrene Books, 2002. This book offers a view of Vietnam and its peoples that goes well beyond the Vietnam War. Its narrative goes back two thousand years, covering the political, social, and military events that shaped this nation.

Thierry Zephir, *Khmer: The Lost Empire of Cambodia.* New York: Harry N. Abrams, 1998. Brief but complete account of the Khmer kingdom, its artifacts, its people, and its sphere of influence. Part of the Abrams Discoveries: History series.

Websites

Hill Tribes of Thailand (www.lisulodge.com). Contains colorful photographs and information on the indigenous tribes of Thailand's hill country, including the Lisu and Karen.

Indigenous Peoples of Malaysia (www.windowstomalaysia.com). Short but informative vignettes on Malaysia's primitive tribes, including the Penan and Bajau.

Karen Home Page (www.karen.org). This home page of the Karen people contains basic information on language, customs, and traditional tribal dress. Includes photographs.

Works Consulted

Books

William W. Bevis, *Borneo Log: The Struggle for Sarawak's Forests.* Seattle: University of Washington Press, 1995. This travel narrative is also an environmental study of logging in Sarawak, an industry that is rapidly stripping the region of its rain forest and endangering the future of the indigenous peoples who make their home there.

Margaret Brooke, *My Life in Sarawak.* London: Methuen, 1913. Margaret Brooke was the wife of Charles Brooke, the second "white rajah" to rule Sarawak in the early twentieth century. Brooke, an Englishwoman, had never seen Southeast Asia until she was brought to Sarawak as a young bride. She and her husband, Charles, nephew of the original white rajah, James Brooke, saw Sarawak through a tumultuous era.

Julian Burger, *The Gaia Atlas of First Peoples: A Future for the Indigenous World.* London: Gaia Books, 1990. Although Burger's focus is global, *First Peoples* does a good job of summing up the issues that confront and threaten indigenous tribes in Southeast Asia as elsewhere. Accessible to teenage readers.

Onofre D. Corpuz, *The Philippines.* Englewood Cliffs, NJ: Prentice-Hall, 1965. A look at the issues that dominated Filipino history, including Spanish rule, Christianity, and the rise of nationalism. Corpuz, a professor of political science at the University of Philippines, authored many journal articles on Filipino politics.

Art Davidson, *Endangered Peoples.* San Francisco: Sierra Club Books, 1993. Lavishly illustrated with accessible text, *Endangered Peoples* sheds light on indigenous and threatened cultures around the world, including the Igorot of the Philippines and tribes of Sarawak, Malaysia. Foreword by Nobel Prize winner Rigoberta Menchu.

Donald W. Fryer and James C. Jackson, *Indonesia.* Boulder, CO: Westview Press, 1977. Fryer, a professor of geography at the University of Hawaii, and Jackson, a professor of modern Asian studies at Griffith University, Brisbane, Australia, create a broad survey of Indonesia, its history, its peoples, and its future challenges.

Jane Hamilton-Merritt, *Tragic Mountains: The Hmong, the Americans, and the Secret Wars for Laos, 1942—1992.* Bloomington: Indiana University Press, 1993. Hamilton-Merritt, who spent years as a journalist in war-torn Laos and lived with the Hmong for a time in refugee camps, details the fate of tribespeople who aided the CIA against the Vietcong during the Vietnam War.

Graham Harvey, ed., *Indigenous Religions: A Companion.* New York: Cassell, 2000. A collection of scholarly studies on indigenous religions around the world, including Southeast Asia.

Mary Somers Heidhues, *Southeast Asia: A Concise History.* London: Thames and Hudson, 2000. The history related in this book is indeed concise, but also complete, covering the entire region from ancient times all the way up to the present.

Andrew Marshall, *The Trouser People: The Story of Burma in the Shadow of the Empire.* London: Penguin Books, 2002. Marshall follows the trek of George Scott, who helped open up Burma to the British. Marshall's modern-day journey puts him in contact with Burmese indigenous peoples as well as takes him to the fabled cities of Rangoon and Mandalay.

Marie Alexandrine Martin, *Cambodia: A Shattered Society.* Trans. Mark W. McLeod, Berkeley: University of California Press, 1994. The history of modern Cambodia, including the murderous Cambodians of the Khmer Rouge, is described by French anthropologist Martin.

Jana Mason, *No Way In, No Way Out: Internal Displacement in Burma.* Washington, DC: U.S. Committee for Refugees, 2000. Paper discusses the ongoing plight of displaced peoples in Burma.

D.R. Sardesai, *Southeast Asia, Past and Present.* Boulder, CO: Westview Press, 1989. Sardesai, chairperson of South and Southeast Asian studies at the University of California at Los Angeles (UCLA), provides this readable yet comprehensive account of Southeast Asian history from prehistoric times to the late twentieth century.

Stan Sesser, *The Lands of Charm and Cruelty: Travels in Southeast Asia.* New York: Alfred A. Knopf, 1993. Sesser's travels through Laos, Cambodia, Burma, Singapore, and Borneo take each country's past as well as its future into consideration.

Tim Severin, *The Spice Islands Voyage.* New York: Carroll & Graf, 1997. Severin sets out on a voyage through Southeast Asia that retraces the steps of Alfred Russel Wallace, the British explorer whose findings greatly influenced Charles Darwin's theory of evolution.

Periodicals

Ethirajan Anbarasan, "Tuenjai Deetes: A Bridge to the Hill Tribes," *Unesco Courier*, October 2000.

Anne De Henning Singh, "Sea Gypsies of the Philippines," *National Geographic*, May 1976.

David Fanning, "Cannibals on Main Street [visiting Asmat people in Irian

Jaya and cruising Indonesia]," *Condé Nast Traveler,* June 1996.

Daren Fonda, "Saving the Dead," *Life,* April 2000.

W.E. Garrett, "The Hmong of Laos: No Place to Run," *National Geographic,* January 1974.

Eric Hansen, "The Nomads of Gunung," *Natural History,* April 1998.

Peter Kunstadter, "Spirits of Change Capture the Karens," *National Geographic,* February 1972.

Newsweek, "Father and Son" (the search for Michael Rockefeller), December 4, 1961.

Thomas O'Neill, "Irian Jaya, Indonesia's Wild Side," *National Geographic,* February 1996.

Eyal Press, "Jim Bob's Indonesian Misadventure: A U.S. Mining Company Clashes with Indigenous Peoples," *Progressive,* June 1996.

Howard Sochurek, "Vietnam's Montagnards," *National Geographic,* April 1968.

George Steinmetz, "Irian Jaya's People of the Trees," *National Geographic,* February 1996.

Greg Torode, "Pulling Up the Poppies," *South China Morning Post,* reprinted in *World Press Review,* June 1996.

Priit J. Vesilind, "Monsoons: Life Breath of Half the World," *National Geographic,* December 1984.

Alan Villiers, "Magellan, a Voyage into the Unknown Changed Man's Understanding of His World," *National Geographic,* June 1976.

Patrick Walters, "Headhunting Again in Borneo," *World Press Review,* May 1997.

Dean C. Worcester, "Non-Christian Peoples of Philippines Islands," *National Geographic,* November 1913.

———, "Headhunters of Northern Luzon, *National Geographic,* September 1912.

Internet Sources

"The Mentawai, Indonesia." www.caske2000.org. Internet journal of a French researcher who lived alongside the Mentawai of Indonesia and chronicled their way of life. Includes photographs.

"Montagnards in the Central Highlands." www.landscaper.net. Includes photographs and articles about the Montagnards during the time of the Vietnam War.

"Montagnards Revisited: In Search of the Past." www.cudenver.edu. Former military colleagues of Vietnam's Montagnards revisit their homelands, only to find their comrades living in poverty.

Index

Picture Credits

About the Author

Author and playwright Mary C. Wilds lives in Indiana. Her plays have been produced in Chicago, and in Cambria and San Luis Obispo, California. Her books include *Mumbet: The Life and Times of Elizabeth Freeman, Raggin' the Blues: Legendary Country Blues and Ragtime Musicians,* and *A Forgotten Champion: The Story of Major Taylor, Fastest Bicycle Rider in the World.*